I Married A City Boy

I Married A City Boy

The Life and Times of an Iowa Farm Family;
Stories to Entertain and Inspire

Karen Schwaller

ISBN: 1546376062
ISBN 13: 9781546376064

For Dave, because you never gave up on your dream to farm, and for the work ethic and agriculture vocations you gave to our children.

The columns in this book first appeared in publications such as
    "Farm News" (Fort Dodge, Iowa)
    "The Land" (Mankato, Minnesota) and
    "The Ames Tribune" (Ames, Iowa)

TABLE OF CONTENTS

SHEEP, TACOS AND WEDDING PANTS

Back when I used to do a lot of wedding photography, I used to wonder why the parents of the bride always looked so exhausted.

All of that wondering stopped when our own daughter got married and we became the exhausted-looking parents of the bride.

The day started out as we would have expected—breakfast, hair appointments and all the usual frantic scampering here and there. In my case, I forgot to bring the orange juice for the mimosas to the hair salon and had to head back to the grocery store while everyone waited to enjoy their cocktails. My bad memory at the start of the day should have been an omen of things to come.

After I returned home, my husband's phone rang and it was a local law enforcement officer. (We really weren't expecting that call until *after* the party...) He asked if one of our sheep was tied up in front of the local Mexican restaurant, which had not yet opened for the day.

The food there is good, but it must have looked ridiculous to see a sheep waiting at the take-out window. She was probably secretly praying there was no sheep taco on the menu.

We had some sheep in a pasture near there, so my husband supposed (without seeing it) that it was ours, and the two of them laughed over the phone about it. Undoubtedly, teenage pranksters at work during the night—catching a sheep, hauling it somewhere, tying it up, and making it home by curfew.

With no practical holding pen at the police department for a sheep, he asked my husband if he could stop by the Taco House that morning and pick it up—which he did, and he returned her to the pasture with the others.

When we finally got to the church (a little late from the sheep circus), my husband announced that his tux pants were too big, and wondered if I could alter them. My sewing machine was at home, and all I had were some safety pins and a needle and thread I had put in a travel bag for emergencies.

There was no shortage of those that day.

I tried fixing the pants in a hallway where there was little traffic, but it wasn't working out very well. They were going to need more work...and I was going to need more of the pants to fix them so the alteration would last all day. So we both entered the men's room, where it would seem a little less out of place for people to see a man in a tux coat with his pants down around his knees. It was there that I began my arduous work.

As I sewed on his pants, a guy walked into the men's room. He looked startled and a little confused. He read the door again and looked at me. I told him to come on in because I wasn't going to see anything. So there I was—in the men's room working on my husband's tuxedo pants—with him still in them--while the door flopped open and shut time and time again ... each time with people seeming startled at the scene that awaited them inside.

And at a church, no less.

By the time the alteration was finished, the professional photo session was almost over, I was sweating, my fingers were bleeding and my spandex body shaper was closing in on me like the jaws of life. Following an earlier outdoor photo session in windy conditions, my hair looked frazzled for the few pictures that were left, matching the looks of my last nerve.

I was a sight.

At the end of the day, the vows were exchanged, the food was eaten, the dancing ensued, the tux pants alteration lasted all day... and the sheep was returned to the pasture.

No wonder the parents of the bride always look so exhausted.

THE TALE OF STAN'S CORNER

Since the invention of farming, many a farmer's wife has lamented over the copious list of tasks to get done when the crop needs to come out.

Certainly, harvest time is the crowned jewel of all the seasons, even though the work load is largely magnified for everyone. As seasons of the year go, farm families tuck a few more in there-- such as planting, baling, harvesting and farrowing/lambing/calving—and the annual dreaded mud season that moves in every spring. That season alone contributes highly to the farm wife's list of housekeeping and laundry afflictions—because it isn't all just mud. And it's part of her reasoning for keeping a bottle of Schnaaps hidden behind the laundry detergent.

With so many seasons that take so much work, it's a wonder that the farm family remembers to get ready for tax season—which takes more pain killers in various forms than any other single season on the farm.

A couple of years ago during the busy-ness of harvest it became evident that I had yet to learn the one thing that all Boy Scouts learn first: think ahead, and be prepared.

I had finished my work and put together a supper for our harvest crew. I now needed to pack it into the car and take it to those who would gather around to eat it under the lights of combines, grain carts and semi trucks.

When I left the field that night I had chores to do when I got home, lunches to pack for our guys for the next day and supper to think about for the next night.

It was then that I noticed the fuel gauge was well on the "E."

I only made it through Blue Birds as far as Girl Scouting went, so apparently my preparedness skills as a third grader lacked in detail and was now mocking me as an adult. And it became evident that the American Red Cross would never see me as qualified to help them in an emergency situation because I would always need gas in the car to get to an emergency site.

While originally I was anticipating my time management once I got home, now I was praying just to get there.

As luck had it, gas fumes (which may or may not have been emanating from inside the car by that time) and a good tail wind got me to a nearby town. It was off the beaten path on my way home, but nonetheless, it was the closest town with a convenience store. The store was called 'Stan's Corner.'

I pulled up to the pump and decided to pay by credit card, considering the limited time I had. I got out, opened the back door of the car and stuck my hand inside to retrieve my purse.

My hand recoiled. There was no purse. Anywhere. A quick assessment of the entire car's contents revealed only food scraps, a sweatshirt, and blankets to put over the seats for dirty farmers to sit on ... and of course, a John Denver CD.

Fat lot of good that did me now.

I had driven from home to one of our furthest away fields with no driver's license, no identification, no gas, and no money for gas.

With no other options on the table, I breathed a heavy sigh, crept into the store feeling a little embarrassed and very frustrated--and asked the woman behind the counter (in an act of blind faith) if I might be able to get a little gas to get me home. After some discussion and a call to the store manager for permission, I got the all-clear for a small amount, and could send the money the next day after I signed away the rights to our first born, considering the price of gas at the time.

I was so relieved that I thought we might name our next dog 'Stan.'

You'd think I'd been at this farm wife thing long enough to know how to keep all of the plates in the air when there is so much to do. It was a good thing for Stan's Corner, a moderately trustful convenience store cashier, the tail wind that helped blow me into town in the first place, and the Schnaaps bottle that helped me be able to laugh about this story when I got home.

THESE CHERRIES WERE THE PITS

There are certain things that the woman of the farm learns as she goes along.

Some of those things are assumed—such as how to cook meals that don't look like they were prepared in a dehydrator by the time her family finally gets in to eat at night; that given the right tools and a pair of gloves, she can do combat with an occupied mouse trap—emptying it and re-loading it for the next ambush; and that timing is everything when barnyard mothers and human mothers clash in an effort to just take care of their families.

It's always an exciting time on the farm—if not exhausting—during those weeks when farm babies are showing up. Checking on impending moms and babies all day long, helping babies get started eating, getting up at night to check them, and not always being able to get back to sleep if you have the middle-of-the-night check. And still working the next day.

I've always been amazed at the manner in which ewes and cows can have their young ones. We've seen them stand there and let the baby come out and plop onto the straw bedding below, then turn around so nonchalantly to investigate what just went on back there.

I've wondered what's gone on behind me plenty of times, but never during childbirth.

If you're helping a cow have her calf it can be quite a production. You want to help the calf land as safely as possible from about chest high, while falling back and doing the fastest backwards scramble ever--to steer clear of all that follows. And for the farmer, the job of seeing the process through isn't complete until everything is out—babies and all the rest of it.

The busy-ness of that time of year leaks over into all of the family, as chores become more labor-intense and time-consuming, and their lives as they once knew them are usually absorbed in all that it takes to expand the herds. There is less time for everything—including meal planning.

A few short years ago when our sons' cows were calving I found myself short on time, patience and ingredients to create a nice meal with all that had gone on that week. When I finally figured out what we were having, I decided to toss together a quick, rich and filling salad by combining some cherry gelatin with some cherry pie filling and putting it in the fridge to set.

When we all finally sat down to supper that night, our sons each scooped some of the salad onto their plates. Pretty soon the "looks" to each other followed, along with muffled snickers as they sniffed and inspected with their forks the salad on their plates. As mothers do, I got my look together that said, "What?!"

One had texted the other under the table to say he couldn't eat it because '...it looked like cow cleanings.'

"I can't eat it right now. Not while we're calving," one of them said to me, trying to mask his urge to burst out laughing and not wanting to offend me.

Oh, for heaven's sake. I wondered how many farm mothers had heard that one.

Of course, I did make that salad again over the years, but not for our family. I knew the conversation that would follow if I set it on the table again, calving season or not.

The year our sons began living on their own I made cook books for them for Christmas, filled with many of the recipes I knew they liked and would actually have time to make as busy bachelor farmers. I included that recipe, if only to bring back a memory that we have all laughed at over the years. I gave it a new name, calling it (appropriately for them), "Cow Cleanings Salad."

I'm hazarding a guess that they've never made it. At least not during calving season.

Timing is everything. And now you don't have to learn it as you go, like I did.

THE NEW WAY TO SLED

There are many things we can learn from farm children—maybe because they are direct descendants from farmers themselves. Children watch and imitate adults—even when they're picking up things we wish they wouldn't.

But farmers are creative by nature. If they can't find what they want—or even if they don't want to pay the price for something they want—they unearth their drawing table, do a little figuring on their blue jeans, lift their seed corn caps to scratch their heads and soon they emerge from the shop, having created something out of almost nothing.

It's what farmers do.

It also reminds me of the story of a man who told God that humans had become so technologically advanced that they could create anything He could create, and they didn't need Him anymore. So God said, "Okay—you can try it. Go ahead and create a tree." So the man reached to the ground to gather up some dirt, when God asked him what he was doing. The man replied that he was making a tree. But God said to him, "No....make your own dirt."

I'll bet God would never make that same challenge to a farmer. He knows they'd do it.

Farmers and their children spend a lot of time together. As often as the farmer has created something out of nothing, the farmer's children have been close by—watching, seeing how it's done, and crafting the trade.

When our children were in middle school, we decided they could spend the afternoon on their own while we had some running around to do. We got a lot done that day—and apparently our children did, too.

Darkness had fallen by the time we returned, and as we drove down the gravel road leading to our farm we could see all the machine shed lights were on. My husband—not one to waste a penny--was already not happy, assuming they had been left on while the kids were in the house. But the closer we got, the more his attitude changed.

We saw something gliding across the snowy front yard behind a four wheeler.

"What in the.........??!??" we both thought as we craned our necks to see what was going on out there. Was that a ... a couch sliding across the front yard? With ... someone ... on it?

My husband rolled the pickup window down, and over the sound of the four-wheeler we could hear the squeals of delight coming from all of our children.

They had created a way to have a little fun outside on a winter day while we were gone. Doing as their dad always did, they went to the shop to see what was around to use to create a sled. They saw a junk couch on a pile somewhere that wasn't doing anything. Now they needed runners.

And once again, the iron pile provided the answer, as it had so many times before for their dad.

"We put some old disk blades on the bottom of the couch so it would slide," said one of our grinning sons as he explained their building process. By now, his dad was grinning, too.

The kids all worked on the "sled" together, then found a rope to hook it onto the four wheeler—and what resulted was an afternoon of bonding in the great outdoors and a whole new definition of sledding. Everyone could participate at the same time, and it offered a new suggestion for 'kicking back and enjoying a cold one.' Their shrieks of joy proclaimed success.

If only the laundry pile held as much excitement as the iron pile does. Shrieks from the laundry room usually mean something totally different. Especially on the farm.

I MARRIED A CITY BOY

Attending ag conferences with your farmer can be a gamble at best.

For the most part I choose to remain in the learning atmosphere instead of joining the band of women shoppers. It's made my husband enjoy the sessions more knowing that what he's trying to funnel into the checking account with smarter decisions and new technology wasn't being drained out with a plastic card somewhere in downtown 'Wherever.'

On the other hand, I once attended a soils workshop that nearly turned me into an inanimate object.

This past winter I was part of a conference session which focused on the succession of agriculture and helping the Midwest to thrive. Part of that was brainstorming about what it will take to bring young people here to live, work and raise their families.

It really intrigued me. Answers ranged from health care laws to infrastructure to the high-speed internet that will be needed for tomorrow's farm families to make it all happen.

But as we talked about the importance of connecting with our millennials and helping them want to—or be able to--return to the farm, I also felt like we were missing an important target group—that being our youngest children. We need young farmers to stay in--or return to—Iowa to take on the challenge of farming and help our industry to be healthy, but I think we need to start earlier in putting that plan into motion. Here's the reason why.

My husband lived his very early years on a farm. He helped with the pig chores and did all the things kids do on farms for work and for fun. He smelled the dirt behind the plow and watched the corn grow taller than him—and as a very young farm boy he thought pigs were pretty exciting.

He was seven years old when the farm they lived on was sold, and his family moved to town. His father began a trucking business and my husband spent a lot of time with his dad in the truck hauling grain, honey, trees or whatever needed to be delivered. It still got him out into the country now and then and gave them time to spend together.

But growing up in town, he always dreamed of being back on the farm. He told me he used to sit in class and draw scale models of hog buildings. (It probably explains his English and history grades.) There were many versions. And he dreamed not only of driving a tractor, but of driving his own tractor someday.

From his earliest memories, the bigger share of his heart was still on the farm, and he always knew it was where he wanted to live his life. When he was 14 he got a chance to have an after-school job as a hired man for a local grain farmer, which lasted all through and after high school. While still in high school he bought a few pigs and eventually a skid loader, putting in the time between high school and starting in on his dream of raising his own pigs.

Financial "starting-out" woes during those early years helped him recognize opportunity when it finally knocked, and he eventually managed his dreams into reality. But the kicker is that--loving it as a very young child made him want to return to the farm when he was old enough to make that decision, even with all those growing-up years of living in town.

Maybe we really need to be reaching out to our youngest for our hopes for tomorrow.

Around these parts, people who don't know my husband's story assume he has lived on a farm all of his life, and are surprised to know he lived less than half of his childhood years there. (He has that 'farmer's blow' down pat.) But for him and others like him, those childhood experiences and memories are where it all started. The seed was planted early. And roots reach down deep.

Sometimes it surprises me to think that in the end, I--a farmer's daughter--married a city boy. Oh, Ava Gabor would have been so proud of me.

WALKING AND WAISTLINE WOES

I wasn't sure if it was misappropriated boldness or if it was the way my coat was fitting me that winter. But one thing was for certain—something was amiss.

As a local news reporter, I'd gone to the hospital to do a story with someone from their public health department. Upon arrival she asked me, "Oh! When are you due?"

"Due for what?" I replied with a pink face, though I knew full well what she meant.

I think we were each a little embarrassed by our own selves at that moment. She apologized and we laughed and got on with our scheduled time together, but her question made me realize that perhaps the cat calls I thought I'd been hearing were really mating calls coming from an approaching wildebeast herd camped a few miles outside of our farm.

I decided immediately that maybe I should begin some kind of diet and fitness routine. I knew it wouldn't be easy, so I thought I better start out slow and do a little walking. I considered running, but there were too many moving parts (front and back) as I did so that led me to believe I could maim myself or someone else if I were to follow someone too closely on the walking trail. It would be especially true in a rollover situation--if I tripped on a fallen tree limb or fell victim to an ill-timed squirrel crossing.

If I'd been much younger with those same moving parts, it could have played to my advantage. But at my age, no one wanted to see it. Actually, I'm pretty sure that even the squirrels would have waited to cross the walking trail until I was out of sight.

And so I began walking each and every day. I also set out to find a bicycle and I did find one at a garage sale. It was blue and had blue fenders and a basket on it, and it reminded me a little of the bicycle Elvira Gulch rode on "The Wizard of Oz." It wasn't much for looks, but the price was right for a stay-home mom on a budget.

As I was examining it, the woman who owned it said to me, "I think you'll really like this bike—it has a nice big seat."

Everyone is a comedian.

As I stood there with the woman and the "Wicked Witch of the West"-like bike, I remembered a time when our (then) elementary-aged daughter was seriously pondering what to be for Halloween. After I had purchased her a witch's hat, she said to me with gleeful anticipation, "Hey Mom! I could use your broom!"

It made that bicycle purchase a little creepy, actually, but I thought as long as I only saw flying monkeys in my sleep, I was probably still close enough to Kansas.

The bike worked well and in time my resemblance to the large circus freak-show lady had somewhat diminished.

Years later as I had stepped up my walking game and got very serious about it, I lost 15 pounds one summer. I was proud of my accomplishment until later that year one of our sons needed to cut some weight for wrestling. It took him all of about three weeks.

Big show-off.

Life was so much easier as a farm kid when weight wasn't an issue. We walked beans all summer long for Mom and Dad and for many of our neighbors. Mom and Dad's seed beans all got walked twice, so there was plenty of unintentional exercise to last the summer.

Oh, how much faster that job would have gone if I could have ridden my broom.

THE BIRTHDAY SURPRISE

Farmers are crafty by nature. I wouldn't say they fall under the "Martha Stewart" category, but they can hold their own when it comes to crafting what they need.

Even if the thing they are crafting is nothing but a smile.

My birthday comes in mid-October—a bad time of year for someone on the farm to have a birthday if there is to be any kind of festival involving members of a farm family. I remember my father telling me once, "You know, you got me out of the field the year you were born." To which I said, "I don't think I did that—I think you did that."

My father—very much a critical thinker--had no choice but to agree with that statement, all things considered, knowing both the birds and bees would back my statement.

I still maintain that it isn't my birthday that comes at a bad time of year; rather, harvest could invite itself each year at a more convenient time.

It's a good thing I grew up understanding that people were always too busy to celebrate my birthday at a time when the farm goes into red alert, calling all hands on deck. And yet, you would think I'd have learned the lesson and married someone whose office was enveloped in smog and was 20 stories in the air, as opposed to being just one step outside his front door.

It must have been a fresh air overdose for me.

This past fall it was setting up to be a typical birthday when our daughter asked me to accompany her on a shopping trip. Happy to have a plan for the day, we headed west.

We went to a few stores, drooled over many things and kept most of our money. Of course, since harvest was in full swing, we made the plan for supper on our drive home and executed it with skilled prowess. We got home at 7 p.m. and split up our jobs. I grilled burgers and loaded them up with all the condiments and wrapped them individually while our daughter gathered up and packed everything else that needed to go along. We backed out of the driveway with supper in tow by 7:20 p.m., with not even one charred burger.

I'm not sure if Ree Drummond or Jesse Owens would have been more proud of us.

When we delivered supper, we stood around talking as always, with tractor and combine lights shining down on us. Soon my husband left and walked toward his truck as I cleaned up the evidence of supper. He soon returned, walking slowly with a bakery cake and some balloons waving in the fall breeze.

I was stunned. One of his trips to the elevator included a stop at the local grocery store that had a parking lot big enough for a semi, and he conducted his secret business there.

I was serenaded by the whole group, who sang "Happy Birthday"— *with harmony, no less* -- under artificial lights. I was bursting with unexpected fall birthday celebratory glee.

Our daughter was an accomplice to the entire plan—which still seemed small compared to the year she orchestrated an entire surprise party on the first year my age started with a "5." It was the closest I ever came to needing smelling salts. Lucky for her harvest went quickly that year, or it would have been only she and I at the party—which would have been no surprise at all.

Happiness doesn't just happen—it's created. And it doesn't matter whether farmers are creating something with the help of the nearby iron pile or a bakery birthday cake. Either way, someone will be happy with the outcome.

Now for a plan to make the banker happy...

THE HOSPITAL WAITING ROOM

I recently had the experience of being in a hospital waiting room while my husband had surgery. Hospital waiting rooms are powerful places. They make you think.

My husband, a farmer who has weathered storms over many years of volatile markets, livestock illness and machinery breakdowns--could not fix this problem. So with a resolve to get it done—he followed the nurse down the long hallway to the operating room.

And I waited.

He was in their care now, and I was amazed by those who had the skills to change lives. Their college days were spent learning how to do that, while I learned how to write a decent sentence.

I remembered a conversation my husband and I had much earlier in the year. As a farm wife, I know my husband carries a tremendous load. He thinks about so many things and makes his very difficult occupation look easy. If I were to start in just on grain and livestock marketing without his guidance, I would embarrass the Annie's Project people who did give me a basic understanding of it. But there is so much more to deal with than we learned there.

He told me once, "If something happens to me, call (So-and-Such) and/or (So-and-Such). They would be able to help you get the grain sold."

They were words that haunted me a little, and yet I've known other farm wives who have been faced with that very situation. I knew I was not deemed exempt from the possibility.

I thought about what it would mean to live my life without him. I came pretty close to it a couple of decades ago when an industrial explosion came inches from taking his life. The man standing next to my husband was called to his heavenly home that night. My husband was not. It happened two weeks after our daughter's third birthday, and just four days before our sons' first birthdays. They would have grown up with no memories of their dad, and would most likely have grown up in town, since there would have been no reason for me to stay out on the farm alone with my very young family.

Over the years I have wondered what kind of children they would have been, and what kind of adults they would be today if they hadn't had the chance to be raised on the farm.

My husband lived on the farm until he was seven--long enough to fill his very young veins with the life blood of the land. He returned there and raised his children on the farm and singlehandedly gave them his same dreams as they grew.

He has always been grateful since the day of that industrial explosion that he got to be part of our children's lives and see them grow into adults who care about the land and those who live there. He gave them a love of livestock, and helped them understand that circle of life that everyone learns from loving animals. Because of his dream, he was able to give them all vocations in agriculture— another of his dreams came true.

People wait in waiting rooms for much more serious issues than my husband had, and I was reminded of that as I saw a children's room in that surgical hospital, along with a chapel.

We were blessed, being able to pass him off into the hands of others who had the skills and delicate abilities to rid him of his pain. They could do more for him than I could as his wife. And for that, I was grateful.

Truly, there but by the grace of God, we go—on the farm, and in hospital waiting rooms.

Both are powerful places.

A VISIT TO THE BARBER

One of the first things a farm family learns is that they need to stockpile the cash reserves—if there are any--whenever they can. Sooner or later we all find out that livestock and grain prices can fall. They can fall hard and they can fall fast.

We first experienced a serious crunch in the 1990s when hog prices went through the floor. When examining the bills and the checkbook, there was no questioning that we had to cut back. One of the first things that had to go was haircuts in town.

I had never cut anyone's hair. The very thought of doing it myself was a little hair-raising, but I figured if my husband wasn't afraid of looking like Lyle Lovett did back in the day, I should not fear the process either. And so I plowed ahead.

I took our two toddler sons to town to get their last paid hair cut from a professional. I brought bags of fruit snacks with me because, of course, they needed something to occupy themselves since they couldn't pretend to be farming while they were sitting in the chair.

The barber clipped and visited while I watched what he was doing. I paid the man, said good-bye and left there for the last time, hoping I had it figured out.

Our boys were small enough that their first haircuts were in booster chairs on top of the kitchen table. A towel and clothespin served as the haircutting apron, and a package of fruit snacks deemed them oblivious to what was really going on. (It seemed a better option than a hairy lollipop.)

Of course, our sons being very young farm children, loved to talk about the farm. One of them in his very young home haircut days, watched as I put the attachment on the clipper, and told me, "That looks like a corn head."

Well, of course it did.

Right from the mind of a farm kid. To this day when I put it on the clipper, I always remember that he thought it looked like a corn head.

The home haircuts continued over the years and they moved off of the kitchen table. A few years later when that same son got a little older and it was time for prom, he once again found himself in the home barber's chair. We were chatting and catching up on his life—when I dropped the clippers onto the cement floor.

"That thing better still work," he said firmly, imagining having to face his prom date with only half of a haircut, or a farm cap with his tux.

Luckily for all of us, it did keep working.

The years have passed, and I have visited with all of our guys about the farm and their dreams; I've heard and talked about their problems, and laughed and listened to their jokes and life stories they have shared with me. I look forward to that one-on-one time spent together.

Recently our sons came over for their post-harvest 'do. The back door popped open and I heard a familiar voice yelling, "Mom? Is the barber shop open?"

It's the one good thing I can attribute to the hog market decline of the 1990s. Lack of funding made me hone a new skill and in exchange, it gave back to me more than I ever imagined, in terms of cultivating important relationships. It happened 20 minutes at a time and all it cost us was a hair clipper. I have been truly grateful.

Sometimes it's hard to tell the difference between hard times and good times.

THE WISDOM OF THE HARVEST

The bible was far ahead of its time in saying, "The harvest is plentiful, but the laborers are few." *(Luke 10:2)* With less than 2 percent of the world's people farming, it would seem they carry a great load in feeding the rest of the world. The biblical statement is as true now as it was when St. Luke wrote that verse, though it was written in a more profound context.

Still, there are many things the harvest as we know it can teach us today:

- **Practice makes perfect.** Learning to operate machinery for the first time can be scary, especially if your age begins with more than a "1" or a "2." But it's important to learn new things. Every day. It exercises our minds and increases our offerings to the world.
- **There is strength in numbers.** One kernel of corn or one soybean may not matter, but billions of them standing together in a field will feed many. Each individual grain adds to the greater cause. Get out and find your cause, and stand with others to see it through.
- **You can only go 'so fast.'** When driving in the field during harvest, ruts, driving over rows and operating a full combine can give plenty of reason to drive slowly, even if we're in a hurry. Slow down and make time to spend time with the people and things in life that matter most. The

sunset is coming and we live in a hurried world; but once that sunset has come, there is no more time.

- **Some days, everyone dumps on you.** This is just as true in the field as it is in life. In the field, combines and grain carts both dump into other venues. It gets the job done. But they each only hold "so much," and if they are over-loaded, bad things can happen. Be aware of how much you can hold, and walk away before you are overloaded and before bad things happen.

- **Grain is more golden when the sun is out.** The morning sun gives grain its most brilliant color. We, too, are more beautiful when our 'sun' is out – when we shine our inner lights before others. Everyone loves the color of gold.

- **Sometimes you have to scoop.** Just as unloading snafus can make a mess on the ground, life can be messy and needs to be cleaned up now and then. Don't be afraid to get the proverbial shovel out, clean up the mess and, most importantly, move on.

- **Mature grain has a lot to offer.** Farmers wait all season long to find mature grain in their fields to harvest. People, too, grow older and with that comes the wis-dom of the ages. Seek out those people, learn from them and harvest as many golden nuggets of wisdom as you can from them. They are all our ancestors in agri-culture, and they know things we don't.

- **Corn stover is opportunity.** Corn stover provides us op-portunity to increase our profits if we want to do the ex-tra work. Don't miss opportunities in life to take things a step further.

- **Windmills just keep on going.** They look so peaceful around the countryside. They don't move fast, nec-essarily, but they move steadily. There is a lot we can learn from that. More often than not, slow and steady wins the race, even if there are hurdles to jump and mountains to climb.

- **Be in synch with the one next to you.** Combines and grain carts have to drive at the same speed down the field and maintain the same distance from each other in order to be successful. Find that person in the world who will walk with you in this crazy journey we call life. Walk at the same speed, and never distance yourself more than necessary from those who care most for you.

- **Lastly, stand close to each other.** Corn stalks and soybeans are planted close to each other. That way they produce the most grain possible and they help protect each other from Mother Nature's fury. In life, stand close to the people you love and protect them. You will be stronger because of it, and you will naturally harvest a bounty much greater than anything man can offer. You will reap a crop of love and gratitude.

And there is no more important, life-giving bounty than that.

MACHINE SHEDS AND KITCHENS

There has probably not been a greater "No Man's Land" than a farm wife walking into her husband's machine shed or shop—especially if he's been working on a big project.

Now and then I'll find my husband out in the shop working on the next big project of the week. I know he's out there from the pounding of metal against iron that goes on and the language I hear muttered following something that did not go well. Luckily, sometimes that language is overruled by the starting of the air compressor that kicks on.

That air compressor could rescue him from embarrassment if our local pastor were to drop by unexpectedly someday while he's working on our International 1086.

Impatiently, my husband might ask me to get him the 7/16 end wrench.

"Where is it?" I ask incredulously, looking as if I was standing in the aftermath of some kind of natural disaster.

"It should be hanging on the wall," he answers, without looking up.

When it isn't there (of course) I may ask again where it could be.

"It's probably somewhere on the bench then...I hope," he says, (along with some words that will give him reason to go to confession on Sunday).

The bench is often knee-deep in the previous project the guys worked on, and in the rush of the season, things may or may not have been returned to their proper place. We may need to look on the floor or out in the yard where the dog may have dragged something that was recently used, holding it ransom in exchange for a little attention and affection.

The female of the human species should take note of that ingenious thought process.

But it's no different for a guy walking into a woman's kitchen, too.

A couple of summers ago as we were freezing sweetcorn, I was cooking some on the stove and baking some in the oven, and had two different timers going to keep me on schedule for which corn was ready to come out of the boiling water and which was ready to be stirred or come out of the oven.

My husband was in the house once as the timers were going off when it came time to stir the oven corn and rotate the blanched corn. One timer went off, and then the other; and he began to wonder if there was some kind of government conspiracy going on under the disguise of cooking sweetcorn.

"It sounds like Mission Control in here," he said, sounding a little concerned.

Luckily, I knew exactly what was going on, and carried on.

The machine shed and the farm kitchen have much in common. Both places can get pretty greasy sometimes; amazing creations are made, large tasks are undertaken, appetites are fed, serious decision-making conversations happen, and both are places where people meet to catch up, have a beverage and compare notes on all kinds of things from child rearing to calf scours to cornering and capturing the wild beast--be it animal or human.

Pickup trucks are often seen gathered around the machine shed as family members come together to work and neighbors come over to borrow things or ask opinions about crops or livestock, and share what's happening with their families. Those same friends and neighbors can be found sitting at the kitchen table, catching up on life or stopping by around the holidays or following a family crisis or hardship.

Some of the most meaningful times on the farm are shared in the machine shed and in the kitchen. And it doesn't even matter whose domain it is.

CROPS AND FARM WIFE BOTH MATURE

I read a post last fall on social media. It said, "My favorite color is October."

A change of seasons is always refreshing, especially when lush green bursts into all the warm colors that autumn produces. I noticed upon late summer this year that the soybean fields were beginning to look as dry as my skin does, and that the leaves were beginning to change color—much like my own hair has done over the last few years.

The soybeans and I have both been maturing, and there are others who have noticed.

Last week I was at the cash register of a clothing store, when the clerk asked me, "You're not over 55 are you?"

"No," I said, sure that Alan Ludden was hiding somewhere in the store. "I'm a few months from it. Why?"

"Well," she said as she looked me over. "We have a senior citizen discount here each Wednesday. You might as well have it."

I was glad to save the money, but was traumatized that someone would deem my face worthy of a such a discount. Apparently I need to either find a new wrinkle cream or pony up the cash for a facelift. (Lord knows what else needs to be lifted.)

On the farm, life changes happen every year. Farm babies are born and others die. Planters come out each spring. Crops go from green and growing to yellowish-orange and slowing down, to brown and dried up. Combines emerge, crops are swallowed up and then heaved out the unloading auger.

Farm families know fall means all hands are needed on deck. Every day.

No exceptions.

There is equipment to keep running and financial decisions to be made for the year based on what the yield monitor says. People are needed to haul grain and bale the corn stover and spread the manure. Livestock still needs to be fed at home while people are in the field, and meals on wheels to be delivered to farmers who have already worked a 12 or 13-hour day by 6 or 7 p.m. For farm families, fall tells the story of decisions made all growing season long.

For young children, fall is a season of great excitement as they see those combines do their thing. A 90-mile trip to my parents' farm one October prompted a new game for our (then) very young children. Everyone was supposed to count the combines in the fields on their sides of the car. Those who had counted more combines in the fields on their side of the car by the time we got to my parents' farm won the game. They stayed occupied the whole time.

I was a genius.

But that was back in my 'green and growing' days of living and parenting. These days I'm somewhere between the stages of 'yellowish-orange/slowing down' and the 'brown and dried up' stage.

Good thing I'm a farm wife and not a dairy cow. That's all I have to say about that.

STREET SMARTS IN THE LADIES' ROOM

Technology has passed me by. And nowhere is it more evident than when I visit the ladies' room at the local "wherever."

A trip to the water closet is supposed to refresh me, and that's what it would do if I could simply flush, wash and dry before I leave. But most often anymore my intellect is challenged by these very basic restroom protocols, and I feel the need to lie down with a cold compress when my experience in there is finally over.

We've come a long way since the outhouse, but honestly, I'm not sure where this whole procedure is headed.

More than once I've gone to flush the toilet, only to find that I have no idea which button or doo-hickey is supposed to get that job done. When I finally figure it out, I'm glad to get on to hand-washing so I can leave, only to find that no water comes out when I wave my hand under the faucet. Finally I reach a faucet where cold water will actually spill onto my hands, and reach for the soap dispenser.

Once again, nothing. But usually there's an eight-year-old a couple of sinks down having tremendous success with this process.

When my hands are adequately dripping, I go to get a towel or have my hands blow-dried like the grand-prize calf at the 4H and FFA beef show. If there is a towel dispenser I find myself examining it as if it's some kind of new life form as I search for the button to push or knob or dial to turn. Sometimes paper comes spewing out if I wave my hand underneath of it—and sometimes not. The hand dryer will either leave you believing you could have blown on your hands yourself and gotten just as much done, or it will nearly rip the skin right off of your hands.

Skinning wild game would take far less time with one of these things.

I spent all those childhood years watching "The Jetsons" on Saturday morning and didn't learn a thing about how to really prepare for my future. At the time I didn't know preparing for my future would involve learning how to flush the toilet and wash my hands. I thought I aced that one once I was out of diapers.

For the farm woman, it's much the same kind of ladies' room dilemma when she finds herself answering Mother Nature's call in the field. Mother Nature simply will not be ignored, and when the nearest latrine is 10 miles away, 'baring it all' is more a term of desperation than it is a high-paying offer from Hugh Hefner or the tabloids. It's a little more complicated for her than simply checking the wind direction. I think there's always a reason our guys know what direction the wind is coming from.

I'd been helping out in the fields here and there for 20 years before another farm woman told me the most efficient way to 'go' in the field. It was a great plan, but it also meant the risk of exposing my backside to whomever might be gracing the surrounding gravel roads--or the field next to ours--since the plan did not involve hiding myself in the nearest tall corn.

Truthfully, I'm not sure I feel all that comfortable anymore even 'going' in the tall corn, because with all of the satellites and drones that can zone in effortlessly, I'm afraid I'll end up on YouTube.

It does take some special talent to make everything go where it's supposed to go AND keep your clothing and the bathroom tissue clean. (Or as clean as it can be after it's been riding around in a dusty bread wrapper in the tractor cab throughout the last four harvest seasons.)

It might still be far less stressful for the farm woman to 'go' in the field than to figure out some of these modern lavatory facilities. And there are no eight-year-olds out there showing us how it's done in the fields, either. After all, we're closer to the outhouse era than they are.

Oh, to just be able to check the wind direction outside when Mother Nature calls.

OF CANCER AND FARMING

If there is one thing we can learn from farmers, it's to keep living your dream even though things don't always turn out the way they should. And in farming—as in life--we can all attest to the fact that there are no guarantees, no matter how much we plan ahead.

Sometimes there is not enough rain, or too much rain; not enough heat or too much heat; not enough time or too much time; not enough help; not enough grain; not enough money coming in; too much money going out; not enough power to help animals regain their health sometimes.

It all contributes to stress on the farm, but as any farmer knows, you meet those challenges head-on and do your best to conquer.

And sometimes you do.

I recently took my mother to her appointment at the cancer center. It's a place where hairless heads, hats and comfortable clothing are the "in" things.

It's also a place where reality slaps us in the face.

My mother's diagnosis of acute large "B" cell lymphoma came in 2011, as she was in her late 70s. But after one year of fighting it, she received the unexpected news of remission. Her last visit was for a check-up, so after her lab work we waited. Would she still be in remission? Would the cancer be there again? After two hours we learned there was no sign of cancer.

Our prayers were answered.

As we were awaiting the results, my mother and I experienced the joy of hearing the bell ring in the waiting room. It was a young woman whose hat covered her hairless head.

You only ring the bell when you have been declared cancer-free.

Immediately, everyone in the waiting room began to clap for her as she began to weep. As she covered her face, her family shrouded her and the hugging began. The applause continued in the waiting area by dozens of people she didn't even know—but who were there for the same reason she was there. They were sharing in her joy. And some of them were wiping tears away, too.

A woman seated in the waiting area went over to her, hugged her and offered words of congratulations. Emotions ran wild. It was plain to see she was exhausted from the battle, but she had received the crowned jewel of news—and she still had a lot of life to live. She and her family left the cancer center, arms around each other, gratefully renewed in spirit. They got into a van that declared on the back window, "Today I have my last chemo."

As I watched this beautiful scenario unfold in such a scary place, I thought about how the life of a farmer and a cancer patient are much the same. Sometimes on the farm we get news that we don't want to be true. We wait things out. Sometimes the news we get is wildly exciting. We fight forces we can't control. Sometimes our emotions get the best of us. Sometimes the news we get is hard to swallow. Some experiences leave a bad taste in our mouths. Sometimes crops or animals don't make it—and sometimes they rally back. The work load exhausts us. Sometimes people don't know how to help us. And we discover we're not in control of everything.

But as cancer patients might tell you, it's worth the effort put into the daily grind of getting through today in the hope of a better tomorrow. Farmers do it all the time--they also know that tomorrow's livelihood is not promised.

But they can still carry the hope—because sometimes, it's the hope that carries them. It's an important part of living the dream, as any cancer patient—or any farmer—can tell you.

THE DIFFERENCES BETWEEN US

It goes without saying that there will always be differences between women. Our likes and dislikes, our shapes and personali-
ties, our taste in clothes, music, food, hair stylists, doctors, home
decor, ingrown toenail remedies, bathroom scale accuracy, laundry soap and more.

But perhaps our biggest differences lie in the way we choose
our spouses, and where that choice takes us. This brings us to the
differences between farm women and their urban counterparts.

Let's start with the laundry. I don't doubt that women in town
have husbands who tend to get into the grease and present her
with the challenge of getting it out of his clothes. Farm women
also deal with that, and the issue of natural fertilizer. I truly don' t
know if urban women have to hose off blue jeans in the front yard
before they get washed, but I know I've had to do it a few times.

The mailman must wonder what goes on around here.

The farm woman knows that supper is served at "dark-thirty,"
and not before. A 6 p.m. meal would serve only as a snack, since
there are at least four more hours of work to do before it gets too
dark—and even then, Thomas Edison's invention allows supper
time to be even later sometimes.

Cleaning the farm house is even different than cleaning the
urban home. While certainly young children and household projects can create messes in any home, the farm woman deals with
ag commodities in her house. Corn, soybeans, alfalfa dust and

oats are scattered on the basement floor from the clothing and shoes of tired farmers who come in late at night--along with acres of dirt from shoes and socks after the guys have been out picking up rocks in the field all day.

The farm mom will even find an occasional sheep's tail taking sanctuary in the basement—a treasure that young hands have discovered and rescued. And if she doesn't find a corn stalk growing in her basement, she's been successful in house cleaning over time.

And the dust. By the looks of our house, historians would scratch their heads in bewilderment over how the Dust Bowl of the 1930s has managed to still hover directly over our farm 80 years later.

There are many babies on the farm—mostly four-legged ones. But many a farm wife can tell you that her own babies will be winter ones, lest she finds herself in the delivery room alone because the crops need to be planted or harvested, or the hay needs to be baled before it rains.

Farm children themselves are even different than children who grow up in town. While urban children know the rigors of household and yard responsibilities, farm kids also know what it is to get out of bed early every morning even during the summer, simply because their animals are waiting to be fed. They learn to operate farm machinery, vaccinate animals, build fences and gates, and work with livestock—sometimes chasing them down country roads and out of fields when they break free.

It's Mother Nature's track practice, which unfortunately knows no age limits.

Only a farm mother has the gall to bring manure-spattered young children in to the house, clean them up for the day and kiss them good-night. Sometimes her husband is the manure-spattered one, and sometimes it's she herself, too.

To the farm woman, red and green are more than just a display of Christmas colors. The banter goes on all year along as to which color dominates in the farm yard.

A young urban girl might hear the words, "Get your boots on—let's go!" and think of a snowmobile excursion or even a shopping event. But that same thing being said to a farm girl doesn't hold the same appeal. She knows it's time to clean out the barn again.

One thing binds us together as women, though—and that is what we see as beautiful. Our urban friends may not see the beauty in a manure-spattered young child, but the farm woman sees tomorrow's food producers in the midst of all of that mess she cleans up each day.

Whether they're from the farm or from our urban population—beautiful adults emerge from both places—even though the process of getting them there are as different as the people who raise them.

NEEDING A VACATION FROM VACATIONS

As farm families go, the word 'vacation' is one that only comes out every few years. When I was growing up it was a word we would have to dust off because it had been so long since we last heard it.

When we heard rumors of it, whispering and sibling networking would ensue as we wondered if it was really true. Would Dad really stop working long enough to do that?

My parents were brave indeed, taking seven kids on vacation in a station wagon. It was a lot of work for our parents to be able to afford it. One way they could make it work was to move in with unsuspecting relatives for the week, but most often we resurrected the old pop-up, pull-behind camper and a tent.

Oh, how our mother used to dislike our camping excursions. Becoming a farm wife after growing up a city girl was adjustment enough. She always said, "All this does is take my job and put it on wheels. That's not a vacation for me."

She did have a point.

She had to stock it with food, cooking and dining pieces, sheets and blankets, cleaning supplies, make sure the camp stove was working, make sure the tent got packed and more---and all of this after she first evicted the mice who had set up shop over the winter.

I'm sure the Department of Human Services would have taken us away from our parents if they had only known.

It was August of 1977 when we left to vacation in some of Iowa's state parks. Dad decided we should see some of Iowa—the only state that grown-up farm boy ever called 'home.' Things went along smoothly until one day it happened. We heard it on the radio and we couldn't believe it. The eyes of my sister and I bulged like Rockerfeller Christmas stockings.

Elvis Presley had died.

We were camping near Boone....and without a television. My sister and I were like fishes out of water. From that point on we couldn't wait for family time to be over so we could get back home to a television that would show us what the rest of the world would be seeing in all the days that would go by until we finally got home.

If there were cell phones and internet back then, we were oblivious to it.

Fast forward many years, when my own family decided to head out to visit some family in Colorado. I prepared and packed everything for us and our three kids. We started out on that long journey during a week when temperatures were in the high 90s and low 100s.

As we drove along, I had the same feeling that the mother on "Home Alone" had when she wondered if she had forgotten something. I remembered all the kids, but still the feeling nagged.

And then it occurred to me—I had forgotten to pack underwear for myself.

My mother made it look so easy—as kids, everyone always had underwear on vacation. Pity that my own children wouldn't be able to make that proud declaration.

A look from my husband told me that he wasn't sharing—especially with those kinds of temperatures and humidity. Desperate times called for desperate measures; there are certain things even husbands won't share—and wives wouldn't want to share.

Underwear stores were few and far between, and time was running out, with stores soon closing for the day. We happened upon one small South Dakota town that had a Mom-and-Pop dime store, and luckily I found some of the beautiful merchandise.

I've never looked at underwear—or vacation preparation--the same again.

Both were great once we were all intact. But I may have needed a vacation from vacations after that.

HAVING IT ALL

A few years ago as I celebrated my birthday with friends at work, someone handed me a beautifully-wrapped package. She wished me a happy birthday and said, "It's so hard to know what to get you because you have it all."

I was quite stunned at her statement, especially since I had always thought the same of her. She was a stay-home mom by choice. She had a beautiful lake home, boat, and even had the time and funds to go to the gym several times a week. She always drove new vehicles and she and her husband owned a time-share in another country.

And she's never even had to power wash a farrowing house out. Ever.

It was shocking to hear that she thought I had it all as a farm woman. Farm people deal with animal smells and manure on a daily basis—inside and outside the house and even (gasp!)---in our washing machines. Vacation time is hard to come by. We get hailed or flooded out some years, and our cash flow shows it. Operating costs are frightening, and any extra cash flow we do have goes back into the business—including the banker. Our livestock depend on us every day to care for them with food, water and shelter, regardless of weather conditions or our own personal crises. Plant and animal health can be time-consuming, especially in light of new diseases.

And learning new technology is necessary in today's ag climate, regardless of how much time or money it takes to accomplish it.

But living on the farm, you also get the chance to see life at its basic core level. Baby animals are born—and leave this earth--in much the same way people do, and our children see that from the time they are very young.

We grow food that feeds, clothes and fuels the world, and we see it progress—literally—from the ground up. We plant those seeds and watch them grow into tall, productive plants that are as strong as they are fragile in the face of Mother Nature. Young children learn the cycle of life and of farming—growing grain to sell and to feed the animals, which in turn, they can sell to feed the world and earn themselves necessary cash flow to keep going.

Our busy season is all year long—as we progress from spring tillage and planting to spraying, swathing and baling, silage chopping, harvest and fall tillage, fall baling, fall fertilizer application, and then to lambing and calving in those often chilly months following Dec. 31. With machinery and equipment preparation and repairs in the midst of that, there isn't much time for leisure.

Television time is scant because there is too much real life happening under our noses. Young children learn more from hunting for newborn kittens in the barn and exploring the farm anyway, and older kids dream about being the one telling other people what to do.

A farm work ethic can only be earned by sweating and freezing through the copious work that needs to be done every day all year long.

At the end of the day, we don't always have great cash flow, the luxuries of a boat, a lake home, time share, exotic vacations, new vehicles, or even much of a social calendar.

But what we do have is a breathtaking country view, the sight and heavenly smell of freshly mown alfalfa, machinery in the shed, grain in the bin, livestock in the yards, family around the table and family around the work that needs to be done. We have our own physical workouts in the barn and on the hay rack; we have hay in the barn, the next generation to teach, and the freedom, peace and quiet that comes with life in the country.

My friend loves her life and she has it all, by my standards. But she was right—so do I.

Mine just looks different than hers.

THE HEART OF A MOTHER

"Children are living messages we send
to a time we will not see."

(JOHN WHITEHEAD)

I've read that message many times, always thinking about my own children and how (if things work the way nature intends) I will not be here with them someday.

I heard once that you don't raise your children to keep them. I also heard from a wise and wonderful Hospice nurse (as my mother-in-law was less than an hour away from meeting Jesus) that we raise our children so they will not need us anymore.

I knew what she was saying, but it really struck something in me.

Mothers are amazing creatures. They play the hand they're dealt, and it's not always the hand they anticipated. But mothers invented the poker face, and they just keep on going.

One of our neighbors told me that a friend of hers gave birth to six boys in seven years.

"She told me that no one was happy to see them come," she said as she chuckled. We can laugh about it, but imagine being that mother. Surely there is a special place for her in some heaven that exists for mothers of a live-in Cub Scout troop.

We owe our mothers a debt of gratitude—not only for the obvious reasons, but also for keeping us kids from killing each other when we weren't getting along. It worked out great because when we grew up, we still had our siblings to be our best friends.

Mom knew.

But life has a funny way of changing the way we look at the people who are most important to us. Like our mothers.

My relationship with my mother (now in her 80s) was pretty typical for all of my life, until she was struck with cancer at the age of 78. I saw my mother—who pushed herself to get through a lot of ups and downs in her life *(including the divorce of her parents when she was growing up)* rise to this occasion, too.

She didn't debate over what to do—she said, "Let's get this going."

It was hard to go to a hospital oncology floor to visit her, to see her feeling weak and often puffy from her medications. She lost much of her hair and didn't feel very good or very pretty—but you have to hand it to a mother who can maintain a sense of calm and humor when life as she knows it goes AWOL.

One day a lab technician came in to draw some blood for the gazillionth time since her long stay there began. She asked if she could use a particular arm, to which my mother replied, "Well— you can, but I think all that's left in there is grape juice."

Once when a nurse was administering chemotherapy, she hooked up a small vial to the tubing and said, "I'm sorry, but this is the one that makes you lose your hair." My mother just smiled and said, "That's okay. What's left doesn't amount to much anyway."

One day as she walked slowly down the hallway with her walker, hunched over and wearing a red hat to announce both her independence and her sense of humor, I could see how much I admired my mother's strength, courage and fortitude to move ahead with something so big, so worrisome and so complex. And at her age.

I was still learning from her.

I would always need my mother. Mom and Dad raised me not to need them when I got old enough to take care of myself, but the heart says there are so many other reasons to need our parents after we're grown.

There are no strings as strong—or as weak—as heartstrings. I know my mother will not be with me someday, but she will live on through me and though my children, and in turn they will proceed into a time that neither she—nor I—will see. They will be living messages from me...from her, and from her mother.

The heart has a couple of pretty important jobs—to beat continuously and to govern us in the ways that make life worth living. And it all began for us, with the heart of our mother.

ALL IN THE NAME OF CORN

Let's be honest. Corn is big business.

And it doesn't even matter what kind of corn you're talking about—field corn, sweetcorn, candy corn, acorns, popcorn, corn chips, corn silage, corn-based fuel, corn sweeteners, DDGs, corn-based plastics and fibers—even the corns on our feet are big business for someone.

I love the tongue-in-cheek joke about the vegetable industry crying over the fact that it didn't further pursue the candy industry's notion to make a sweet confection named and designed after kernels of corn. Even so, I wonder what kid (or even grown-up) would purposely consume candy broccoli?

I'm sure there's a reason that never caught on.

Whether the consumers of corn have two legs or four, it seems there's a certain amount of appeal that corn holds to them, because corn affects our lives in a lot of ways.

For the farmer it's a livelihood and a way of life to pass on to children. It's the miracle of new life happening in plant fashion—and when those plants begin to emerge from the black gold that is rich Iowa soil, there is great pride in seeing those just-visible rows of green that hold the future of the farm family within its new and very tender roots. Dreams take shape as the corn grows, and financial decisions are made as the combine rolls across fields of gold.

For a young farm kid, a little corn can produce a vast amount of entertainment. Toy wagons are filled with it via toy elevators, which dump the golden kernels into the wagons below while they watch "Sesame Street." It's good experience for children, who will most likely do the real thing someday, with elevators powered by more than a hand crank.

I remember playing in the corn when we were growing up. Back then we didn't know or understand the dangers of playing in grain bins or wagons, and we did it all the time. Thank God for today's knowledge of the safety issues related to playing in grain.

We used to head out to the corn crib on a hot summer afternoon, climb that very tall, straight-up-and-down ladder that took us to the overhead bins, and jump into that waiting pool of wonderfully cool corn that was up there. You could burrow in up to your neck if you wanted. Only a farm kid can know how much fun that could be. It was a great way to cool off when you lived out in no-man's land, many miles from a municipal swimming pool.

It's a wonder we survived growing up in the 1960s and '70s with little adult supervision. Parents just knew we were out playing somewhere on the farm. I guess we were the original "Children of the Corn."

A few years ago Hollywood created the story of an Iowa farmer who kept hearing a whispered voice saying, "If you build it, he will come." He not only heard the voice distinctly, but pursued it against the wishes of his bankers--and with judgmental looks from his peers, family members and people in his community.

Most all farmers follow the very same logic--if he builds it (the farm and the dream, that is), there's a chance that his children will follow him. His quiet whispering is there for the hearing—if only his children will pursue it.

By the end of the movie we understood the majesty of an Iowa corn field when one of the movie characters asked, "Is this heaven?" And the farmer replied, "No. It's Iowa."

How does Hollywood get off comparing being in an Iowa corn field--to being in heaven?

Just ask any corn farmer. They'll tell you it's real.

Now that's big.

STOKING THAT WINTER FIRE

When the combines and tillage equipment shifted into permanent park mode in the fall of 2014, it came just in time for winter to set in. With harvest starting so late, the snow and freezing temperatures arrived the day after our guys fell comatose from an entire week of running the disk ripper literally around the clock, trying to beat Old Man Winter to the starting line.

It was a victory, though perhaps only a hollow one—with winter as our prize.

But as ironic as it sounds, it's sometimes those cold winter winds that bring us some of our best family memories. I'm not talking about the cutting of wood to stoke the wood stove, family ski trips or afternoons when the kids go outside to build forts in the snow—though those memories are priceless. I'm talking about those cold winter winds that zap our power lines and help us realize how helpless we are without electricity and without each other.

I remember once when I was working at a small-town newspaper. An ice storm had ravaged the area and left us without power. I had been out getting some pictures on that cold, gray morning for the front page and when I returned to the office I flipped on the light switch, but no lights. Oh yeah—no power. So I traipsed to the bathroom to take care of a little business, and when I got in there I flipped the switch again—oh yeah, no power. Some things just aren't going to wait so I finished up my business in the dark and went back to my desk, where I thought I would hear what they were saying on the radio about the storm. Once again, no power. After that I thought I may as well get started writing the story about the storm, so I sat down and pushed the switch to turn on my electric typewriter.

I had to have been one of the first known and youngest local Alzheimer's cases.

I hadn't realized how dependent my life was on electricity.

I also think about times when the power goes out on those long winter days at home. When we had young children around, it used to be a mixed-emotion thing when the power went out in the evening. It never happened at a time that was convenient, but once I got over that, we would all gather around with any flashlights that actually worked, and some candles and blankets. Everyone could have been bickering up until the minute the power went out, but once the darkness fell over us and everything was eerily silent, everyone came together--maybe a little spooked by such saturating darkness, and being glad we all had each other.

It would always take me a few minutes to wrap my head around the fact that I had to stop what I was doing and readjust to the situation. Though at first it seemed unproductive and annoying to have to stop my life and wait for the power to come back on, after a while it was kind of nice to have a reason to stop and relax, to have everyone together--wrapped in blankets as the house cooled off, in the shadowy light of candles and flashlights, with nothing to do but be a family. Stories would be shared as shadows flickered, laughter would ensue, real talking would be done and bonding was happening whether we realized it or not.

Our hog buyer was out one evening delivering holiday goodies when the power was out. It was a new experience entertaining him by candlelight.

We hoped he didn't get the wrong idea.

When those power crews did their thing and the house lit up again, I would have to admit that I was always just a little disappointed at first. Kids scattered to resume their activities, and I was left secretly wishing we would have had more of that time together.

Someday they will understand the heart of a mother.

Stoking the fire in the wood stove to warm the house is just as important as stoking the fires of family—no matter what form it takes—and no matter what the season. There is warmth to be found in family and friends—even in those cold, dark days of winter.

Especially when the power is out.

WHEN CHRISTMAS HIT THE FAN

To say the holidays can be stressful is like saying hogs will find the one and only small weak spot in a fence to get out, but won't be able to see the gaping, huge doorway of a building when you go to chase them back in. It's the infuriating nature of the beast.

The nature of the Christmas beast is the "to-do" list, usually reserved for the woman of the family. There is shopping, baking, Christmas cards, letters and pictures to take and order; gift wrapping, setting up the tree, holiday meal shopping and preparation, house cleaning, decorating the house and tree, coordinating family gathering plans and, of course, looking like you just stepped out of Vogue Magazine. All of this on top of full time jobs, families and weekly activities.

No wonder Grandma got run over by a reindeer—she probably couldn't take it anymore.

We moved into a new home in December of 2013, which was great. Our mistake was moving into it the week before Christmas.

There was so much to do at that time--finishing up the house so we could move in, selling my brand new book, speaking engagements to honor, moving, Christmas and all that goes with it (see above), and getting together for our children's birthdays—which all happen to fall in December.

Our children—all grown up now—were asking when we were going to (at least) get a Christmas tree. The more time that passed, the more it became apparent that there would be no tree other than the one we have in our living room all year, which we decorate for various holidays. We simply didn't have the time for Christmas.

There was no decorating the house, we hurried through the Christmas card ritual and took no family photo to include with the cards. That year we received a Christmas card from some of my family in California with a note that said, "We sure enjoyed your Christmas card, even though it wasn't signed and there was no letter."

Good heavens ... I wondered how many I sent out that way.

Even the Saturday holiday baking date was scrapped in the name of getting everything else done. We were planning Christmas and children's birthdays between two houses. Our daughter was less than impressed.

One evening a few days before Christmas when I brought over the umpteenth carload of goods, I saw that she had parked in front of my garage stall. I wasn't happy, since she knew we were busy moving and needed to get in and out of the garage.

I parked next to her truck, carried my attitude into the house and as soon as I opened the door, demanded, "Do you think you could move your truck so I can get this stuff in the house?"

As I rounded the corner into the living room, there it was— and there they were. Our daughter and one of her brothers, with a fresh Christmas tree they had cut and purchased for us. It was in the tree stand and they were putting the lights on it. They stood there quietly, just looking at me.

I had just done my best impression of the Grinch. And the green skin I was wearing didn't complement my persona in any way. I was a little embarrassed.

I had completely lost track of the reason for Christmas in the rush of all the things I had going on in my life. Christmas is about the ultimate birthday; but just as much, it's about stopping to recognize and appreciate the people who give our lives meaning and purpose. I had forgotten, and in that simple way—without making demands--our children reminded me.

While it wasn't a Christmas out of the Martha Stewart magazine, it was still nice to be all together on Christmas Eve and Christmas Day, with nothing to do but be together as a family.

It really is a wonderful life.

SNIFFING THE FARM

Farm families have, for generations, been a people of great tolerance. After all, there are so many things to tolerate—weather, markets, bugs that work hard to kill your crops before they can be harvested, farm animals with their own plans, machinery that breaks down at the least convenient time, and visitors asking you if you've been saved, to name a few.

But something farm families tolerate the most are the smells that come with the job.

I maintain that only a farm mom would pick up a pair of compression shorts from the floor of someone's room during wrestling season, give them a suspicious whiff to determine the caliber of cleanliness, and with the flick of the wrist, decide what to do with them. Even if they're not clean, she's smelled far worse than that in her role as the woman of the farm.

How I remember the days of working in the hog house and farrowing house. It didn't matter if you were in there two minutes or two hours—you smelled the same either way when you left. Those clothes make their way to the house eventually to be washed—or to be worn a few days more and washed later (coveralls), and so even the farm wife who doesn't work alongside her husband with the livestock still gets a good dose of what he smells all day long.

If we can turn a blind eye to ignore obvious things going on around us, then the farmer is good at turning a blind nose to those smells that would otherwise send a skunk scampering for nose plugs.

There are certain unmistakable smells—such as manure. The farm family can tell the difference in the aromas between the manure of all farm animals—a talent that I'm sure will be worthy of its own reality show someday. They know the smell of rain—and can smell it when it's coming, let alone bask in its smell after their crops have been watered; and they know the smell of death. Hardly a farmer goes career-long without death loss.

Around here we're trying to outsmart a skunk that has decided to plunk down roots and homestead. I was feeding the cats in the machine shed recently and as I was watering them, I looked underneath the hay rack and saw that familiar white stripe not 10 feet from me. I'm not sure who was more surprised, but I was thinking that the wrestling-clothes gym bags I smelled over the years would be a tiptoe through the tulips compared to what I was about to do in my unmentionables at that moment.

Farm families are part coon dog. They've been known to do battle with all kinds of four-legged beasts, but especially rodents around the grain bins. They can smell a rat a mile away and come up with all kinds of concoctions to catch them. Sometimes the rats they smell are two-legged ones. Something else to tolerate.

Daily walks are part of my lifestyle. And in the summer time you can hear the corn growing out in the fields. During the fall when the corn is golden, crisp and being gobbled up by combines, you can smell it on those walks. It's a little slice of heaven.

I went out to the sweetcorn patch one day last summer, and was pleasantly surprised for once by the smells I encountered as I made my way there and back. I could smell the field corn and then the sweetcorn as I picked and husked it. As I made my way back to the house I could smell the sweetness of the nearby alfalfa hay bales, and as I passed the machine shed I picked up the aromas of grease and exhaust fumes, as the guys were working on a tractor.

Some days our guys tolerate the smell of dinner; good thing for that blind nose.

Yes, there are farm smells that are less than desirable, but tolerating them is worth the chance to get to smell those really great ones. It's like getting the last gift under the Christmas tree.

People with big noses—be proud. We may smell more of the bad stuff, but we also get to suck up more of those great farm smells that help make life worth living. And that womps.

A CHILD SHALL LEAD US

Every now and then humor takes a holiday, and the realities of life settle in.

While it's not an unusual occurrence, sometimes the teachers of those realities are what take us by surprise. It's been said that, while we try to teach our children all about life, our children teach us what life is all about.

Our son learned such a lesson not long ago.

He had just returned home from a day of corn chopping. When he came through the doorway of our home, I asked him how it went. He sighed, sat down and said quite factually, "It was an emotionally tough day."

He had been hauling with a truck, and the corn belonged to the friend of a friend, who had died earlier that week. A few friends had gathered together to harvest his corn silage on the day after he was buried. Others there knew the man who had died; our son did not—but our son felt good about helping with such an important harvest.

Awhile into it, he saw a young girl who looked to be about 10 years old--in the yard. She approached his truck and asked if she could ride with him. Happy to have company, he invited her in.

Turns out, she was the oldest child of the man whose corn he was helping to harvest.

She told him her name, and followed that a little later with, "My dad died on Monday."

Our son found himself face to face with a young girl who had experienced so much in her short time on earth, understood the brevity of this life, and who had to find a way to work through her father's illness and death. And possibly, find someone to talk to about it.

She chose our son.

He discovered there were three younger siblings, whom he learned about during the course of their time together. He also learned about some wonderful things the father did for her and their family before he had to leave them behind. Among them, she was especially proud that he built the children a chicken house for their county fair poultry projects, and he bought her a calf to show at the fair.

Our son loves cows and calves, and could relate to how special that calf must be to her.

As they visited, she said, "God must have really liked my dad to take him so early."

Our son said he was trying to think of something comforting to say, but most of all, was trying to hold himself together for the sake of the young girl, who had been dealing with her own emotions about this for as long as she had known about her father's illness. She was doing well, it seemed. She was leading that conversation.

I fought back tears of my own as he was telling me this amazing story of a young girl who reached out to a total stranger and introduced him to her father in the only way she could do that now. And what a job she did. It gave his job there even more special meaning.

I thought of all the amazing people she must have had in her life helping her through something that is so difficult even for adults to understand. Of all of the man's children, she would remember him the most. I thought about the tremendous gift that will be for her.

For one day, farmers banded together with equipment and manpower to harvest a silage crop for a friend. They may not say it, but farmers all know the brotherhood they share, strangers or not. They don't even have to say it. And in someone's hour of need, they're there--even if only to be a sounding board, giving a child a chance to let someone get to know her dad.

Perhaps that was the most important job of all that day.

THAT'S NO BULL

S ome days I don't know what in the name of Gertie's garter goes on around here.

It started out as a normal day. My husband was working on a shed he was building, when his phone rang that afternoon--as it does at least five gazillion times a day.

It would make me crazy.

Pretty soon he traipsed up to the house with a small power tool and asked if I would take it over to our son, who had just called asking to borrow it.

"He said the bull has his head stuck in something," my husband said.

So as farm wives do, I dropped what I was doing and headed over to where our son was to give him the tools to set the bull free from his bondage. As priorities go, freeing a bull trumps mending blue jeans, even though there would probably be more of those to mend after the emergency bovine rescue attempt—whether the mission succeeded or failed.

Mission Control had officially been notified.

I was halfway there when our son called to say he didn't need the tool anymore, that the bull was free. I turned around and went home, and everyone went about their day.

Later that evening the lady of the farm where the bull was staying was telling me how funny it looked seeing the bull with his head stuck, and said she would send me the video she took while out surveying the situation with the guys.

Turns out—unknown to us, the bull had his head stuck in a tree trunk.

You heard me. A tree trunk.

I'm certain I would have been the 'Doubting Thomas' back in biblical days, where I would need to see it to believe it. But there he was in living color—a bull's big, bulky body sticking out from a tree trunk, his tail swinging as if it was just another day out in the pasture.

It was funny to watch the video of the guys working together to free the bull's head from such a ridiculous make-shift trap. Actually, he looked very Winnie-the-Pooh-like.

Trying to imagine what he had been thinking to get himself into this predicament, we guessed he was investigating what a hole in a tree trunk could offer for food or excitement, and perhaps he got a little more of the latter than he bargained for.

It had to be hard on his ego.

I've heard of people with their heads stuck in the sand—and even in specific anatomical locations--but even this was more than I could believe, seeing it with my own eyes.

We watched the brief video with fixed fascination and muffled giggles. We gazed at the two guys working on the tree, carefully monitoring the bull's reaction, and working slowly, methodically and mechanically to open up the part of the tree that enveloped the bull's head.

Inventors continue to improve the way we catch household mice today, but Mother Nature came up with her own way to catch a bull—and without as much as a rope.

Our other son posted a picture of it on Facebook with the caption, "This is the luck we have." And he's right—if your last name is 'Schwaller,' you'll find yourself in some of the damndest situations. It's a guarantee that comes right along with the name.

Just as humorous were the comments that came from others who saw the photo. One said, "I hope his offspring are smarter, or you'll be busy next summer." Our daughter commented, "I think the herd genetics could use some attention."

It was just another typical day at the Schwallers'. And that's no bull.

THE GREAT AMERICAN TRACTOR RIDE

It's always interesting to watch an antique tractor ride—not only for the tractors, but for the stories and memories they evoke. And if you're lucky enough to watch an antique tractor ride with someone who farmed with those tractors, the event seems to come to life.

Our local FFA chapter sponsors a ride every year around the shores of West Lake Okoboji. It gives a glimpse of the "other side" to people who may have never known how it feels to climb onto a tractor and start it up, or smell the dirt those tractors wake up each spring.

We watched some of those events with my father-in-law, who farmed with some of those older tractors. The tractors were as different as those who used them. As they went by, he watched in silent remembrance, and other times, he would share a story.

As one tractor went by he said, "My back hurts just watching that guy ride on that seat."

When he saw a Case-O-Matic in the line-up, he said he remembered calling that tractor a "Jerk-O-Matic," since he thought it was hard to put into gear smoothly and gently.

A tractor with an umbrella went by and he remembered a family friend who had upgraded to getting an umbrella on his tractor. Shade on a tractor was a big deal in the day.

"He said he had to put his over coat on because he got cold," my father-in-law remembered with a quiet laugh, as he took it all in.

My husband and his father tried to remember when and how the Massey-Harris and Ferguson companies came together as they watched those tractors rumble past. We tried to discern what kind of tractor went past us once, since there was far more rust on the entire unit than there was paint. Finally, as the driver went past, we saw a hint of the word "Oliver" on the back of his tractor seat.

Other tractors were shined up with chrome, straight pipes and American flags, and otherwise had their Sunday clothes on, and they ran right alongside those whose tractors wore their work clothes for the day. Iowa Secretary of Agriculture Bill Northey participated in some of those rides, and would drive a work-clothes tractor. It was cool to see.

I was also struck by the fact that, as we sat and watched those tractors drive by, those driving them were usually the first to wave. But then, that's the friendly way farmers are.

There were so many things to take in—the people driving the tractors and taking us all down memory lane. Well, some were taken down memory lane, and some young farmers were proud to drive something their grandfather once used, and others watched and imagined how their grandfather could have farmed with a tractor like that.

There was the sound of the tractors—some were real putt-putts and others were smooth as butter. It's always an exciting time as the ride begins, and the tractors all start up. It's a sense of pride that I can't explain, but it's there, and its' very real.

There are the families of the ride—farmers of every age, wanna-be farmers, women, and young children who are there grooming their love of the feel and the sound of an old tractor. For young children it's great fun; for their families, it's the very future of their farms.

When the ride was over, I was asking my husband's aunt if she had seen that old, rusty Oliver. She laughed and said it reminded her of a Cherokee County man who drove an old tractor like that in regional rides. She told me he put a sign on the tractor that read, "She may not be pretty, but she puts out."

You gotta love farmers and their sense of humor........and the desire of a father and son to share the experience of a simple tractor ride together.

COW CHIP BINGO

There are certain things farm wives and mothers do just because they carry that title.

They carry feed and water pails, field suppers on the go, children, dustpans full of corn, soybeans and alfalfa; sick animals, veterinary supplies, their share of the work load in the house and on the tractor, a few burdens in the not-so-great commodity pricing years, lots of financial responsibility and even a few grudges now and then.

I really thought I had done all of the things that farm wives and mothers have done for hundreds of years, aside from making head cheese and washing our clothes on a rock down by the river.

Our local high school had its Homecoming activities a few weeks ago, and in keeping with the tradition that our FFA chapter started—wanting to be part of the Homecoming festivities and raise a little cash for the Homecoming committee—they once again hosted their annual "Cow Chip Bingo."

Our sons have taken care of providing the "chips" for the last few years, hauling the cow into town and setting her free on the pre-fabricated grid on which she was to do her business.

When you're a cow, all the world is your bingo pad.

With harvest starting late that year, our sons were a little busy trying to keep everything going once they were in the field. Every farmer knows that the window of opportunity sometimes closes quickly when extracting the crop—as many farmers found out that same spring as they tried to plant that same crop.

That's where I came into the picture.

One of them called me up that Friday afternoon to explain what was going on, and asked me if I could haul one of their cows into town so the Cow Chip Bingo could go on as expected that night.

It would've been fine if I had any prowess whatsoever in backing up a livestock trailer.

Passing the buck, I called up the local FFA chapter advisor and pleaded my case after none of the neighbors answered their phones. Was there someone who could come out to our farm and back the trailer up to the gate? I could get the cow chased into the trailer, but the trailer had to be in place first.

Thankfully, he knew of someone who could help—one of his FFA members who, like our sons, could do it in his sleep. He backed the trailer up to the gate in about 15 seconds—first time—and emerged from the truck emotionally unscathed.

I would have spent two hours trying to accomplish that same task.

We loaded the cow and headed into town, where people were interested in her business end.

I was met by the athletic director, who came out to the grounds, smiling, and said, "When she does her thing, just let me know which square gets most of it."

Sure thing, big guy.

She roamed around for a few minutes, looking at the people who were watching her and wondering what all the fuss was about. Finally, she did what she came to do—not even knowing she had made the person who gambled on G-9 a very happy person that night. She just did what cows do out in the pasture.

As I was heading home I got a call from the guy who had been at our house doing some measuring for counter tops, saying he had finished up his work there.

The cow and the counter top guy had both finished up their business on that Friday night.

I apologized for not being there, telling him I was on the way home with a cow who had put Cow Chip Bingo in the books again for this year's Homecoming.

I've never heard someone laugh so hard. Yes. A good, long, breathy belly laugh. It even made me laugh. He'd never heard of such a folly.

Yes, farm mothers—be proud. Cow Chip Bingo would not happen some years if you weren't around. Someone else gets the cold, hard cash, but for us it's the prestige of making it happen.

Be jealous, city ladies.

THE FARM MOM'S JOB DESCRIPTION

It's been awhile since I read Erma Bombeck's take on all that God put into the creation of mothers. From my own perspective, mothers have plenty packed in there to equip themselves to take on that 'mother of all jobs,' literally.

They have to have just the right mix of wisdom to keep the family running, culinary expertise to keep everyone fed, athletic tendencies for traveling with babies and toddlers, coping skills from the delivery room through college graduation years, spirituality to understand why she was called to this freak show she calls her family, and has to have 'the look' down so her children know when they've crossed the line.

And not necessarily in that order.

But ladies of the farm—have you ever thought about all the 'extras' that you have to have in order to be a farm mom? It's a special-order thing. Certainly, if anyone read the job description, no one would volunteer for it unless they saw Dr. Kevorkian sitting in the driveway so he could help you end it all if it takes a serious turn south.

She must be able to run a household on a farmer's budget, keep a large garden because some years it's necessary, and switch roles from farm laborer to farm wife and mother in the blink of an eye.

The farm mother must be able to lift hay bales, the spirits of her family, and the implement behind her as she works in the field.

She should be able to drive livestock, tractors, grain trucks and her children to the doctor after stepping on rusty nails in the grove. Backing up while using mirrors is over the top.

She'll need to be able to do the chores when her guys are all in the field, and know how to take care of loose livestock—whether it's a gate-related thing or a gastric issue. Sometimes those chores start at 10 p.m. when her work is finished as well during busy times of the year.

She should be able to run a simple garden hose for livestock watering purposes--and to wash evidence of livestock off of blue jeans before they go into the washing machine. She must understand that her washing machine will not look pristine, and will see more pliers, rocks and pocket knives run through there than Elizabeth Taylor has had husbands.

She should be able to prepare meals for a crew after work and keep them warm for hours as she hauls them out to the fields in the fall, then come back home, unpack it all and prepare lunchbox lunches for everyone for the next day. She should also be able to exercise restraint when her husband tells her at 11 a.m. that there will be extra people there for dinner.

She should not be afraid to kiss her young children goodnight, when they were covered with manure and smelled like the hog house just an hour earlier. And she should understand that sometimes she will smell like the hog house and walk out of her boots in the manure, too.

The truly amazing farm wife can load hogs without loading up on valium first, and should be able to vaccinate more than just a practice orange.

She must be able to write out the cash rent check with nerves of steel during those years of uncertainty, and sign her name on bank loan and FSA papers with the verbal understanding that she is not signing away the rights to her first born.

She should be able to comfort her young children when sometimes the only thing that can be done to help an animal is to euthanize it. It's just one of those things in life.

But most of all, she needs to understand how closely her husband is connected to the land...because as her children grow, she'll find that the apple doesn't fall far from the tree.

Without farm moms, there is no next generation of farmers. The farm mother is truly a miracle on earth—right next to heavy duty laundry soap. Thank God for both.

THE NEW WONDER LIQUID

There are certain things you have to read that make you wonder how much time will pass before you become literally petrified. We were thinking of getting a computer once and I was doing a little reading about gigabytes, processors, RAM, modems, sound cards, video cards, monitors and motherboards. After reading all of that, I was certain that I would not be able to tell anyone that much useful information about any of our children, and I even helped manufacture them.

But every now and then you run across something that could change your life. I read such a paper this week—one that told me I don't have to hide the vodka in the empty gravity flow wagon in the machine shed anymore.

Every farm woman has her breaking point.

The article said I could bring it into the house and use it openly and shamelessly there—for household improvement purposes. And if there was ever a house that could use improving, it's the farm house.

The article said I could remove household and clothing odors with a few spritzes of vodka, since the alcohol in it kills bacteria which cause odor. I wonder if anyone in the test lab walked into the boot room after the guys have been out hauling manure, or after someone has taken an unintentional bath in diesel fuel and comes into the house or garage to change. The paper said we could spritz our clothing and hang them in a well-ventilated room. I think we needed the well-ventilated room long before we needed the spritzy deodorizer.

I read that it works well to get rid of flies and other pests—that you can spray it directly onto them and it will drop them like.... well, flies. There is no other house that has more flies than a farm house, especially if there is livestock around. Though I would assume a person's aim might not be as sharp after a squeezing few spritzes and breathing in the mist, it could make ridding the home of flies a much more enjoyable job.

The article said slipping an ounce of vodka into shampoo can make hair lush and bouncy. It must have the same effect on hair as it does on people. This, I'm thinking, could be good news for sheep and calves in the wash racks at the local county fairgrounds. Who wants to show an animal whose hair isn't as lush and bouncy as its owner's?

Further down it said I could use vodka to treat stubborn stains if I splashed a little of it on one and applied a little elbow grease before laundering. It would be my luck that the elbow grease wouldn't come out, either.

The article said I could use it to get rid of weeds. It said vodka attacks broadleaf weeds by breaking their protective coverings, leading to death by dehydration. I can imagine using this one in the garden, but what if the idea was taken on by farmers, filling their sprayers with it? Imagine the drift—and how happy farmers would be to mix a little work with a happy attitude.

I also read where I could use it as an ingredient in homemade mouthwash. If successful, the farm woman would be more than pleased to vow to always have fresh breath no matter if she's power washing the farrowing house or sewing a new zipper into insulated coveralls. That last job might require a certain amount of vodka to accomplish, anyway.

For now, keeping it out in the machine shed is probably the best case scenario. What would my mother-in-law think of me if she opened the cupboard and reached for the laundry soap, only to find a bottle of spirits there?

Maybe she would wonder if her own bottle from home was missing.

FARMER STRONG

If you even know a farmer, you know what I'm talking about. There's a certain kind of strength that belongs only to a farmer. And if the rest of the world understood it, there would be a national day of recognition for those who choose to spend their lives filling our plates three times a day, every day.

You may know a farmer if you've ever smelled him coming before you were aware of his presence. Though it's not always that way, you'll want to admire his strength from a distance after he has spent the day power washing the hog house or scooping rotten corn out of a bin. You may also want to give him a snack that comes with a wrapper or a fork on those days--his hands may not be the cleanest. And you may want to distribute it at the end of a long stick.

The farmer is a man-beast of sorts. He can heft heavy hay bales straight up, not even needing that familiar "bale swing space" to get it where it needs to go. He can carry four hay bales at a time across the yard. While his slow and paced stride in doing so may resemble a penguin mother-to-be, he knows how to get that job done when he's the only one there.

A farmer can pick up one end of a 250-pound pig on hog loading day. Of course, this depends on how well the hog loading is going. The madder the farmer, the lighter the pig.

The farmer has hands strong enough to crack open pails of feed additives, hook up heavy implements and fix motors, and gentle enough to cradle a tiny, sick lamb.

He scales the sides of grain bins and silos with great athletic prowess—sometimes, holding a shovel as he goes. That should be a new Olympic sport. There are times when his wife's heart is racing as much as her farmer husband's is by the time he reaches his destination. It's a long way to the top going straight up, and a short way down if his foot slips.

He bales on the hottest days of summer and repairs frozen livestock waterers bare-handed when it's twenty below zero. He's out checking pregnant livestock, delivering baby animals in the middle of the night, and works around the clock to get the crops out and the last of the fall tillage done before it freezes.

Straight rows and healthy crops are important to him; after all, everyone will see.

He sits with a pencil and a calculator as he markets his commodities, and does so with a stomach of steel as he plays that game. He fills out his financial statement for his banker, and sometimes wonders why things weren't better, based on how hard he worked all year.

He watches his children struggle with the death of animals they've grown close to, and even struggles with it himself now and then. He watches his young children clumsily learn how to run his equipment, sitting next to them, guiding and encouraging— sometimes with firm tones. But always, teaching the next generation how to do it after he's gone.

He shoulders years when commodity prices convince him to put off buying needed equipment, and spends money cautiously in the good years, knowing it may not last.

His skin is leathery, calloused, lined and worn—not only from Mother Nature, but from years of worry, a few years of hardship, and a lot of sleep deprivation.

And yet when that sickly motor runs like a top again at the work of his hands, when healthy animals greet him at the feed bunk, when he successfully crafts a machine part out of scrap iron because he can't afford to buy new; when he can fix something himself, when he stands in his field and feels the rain water his crops...when he puts on his cap and squints in the sunshine of a brand new day, it's enough to give him the guts to do it all over again.

Now that's farmer strong.

SHOVELING IT OUT

O ne of the first things farm kids learn about is that animals get hungry and need to be fed. It might start out with them feeding the dog and cats, but eventually winds up with them carrying feed pails to hungry hogs and sheep, and then driving the tractor and feed wagon to fortify a group of waiting cows.

What a transition it is to watch.

Farm children seem to be born with a shovel or a bucket in their hands, and they make up their own schedule of uses for such dad-like tools. They may include sandbox digging, kitty transportation and digging holes to bury treasures like lamb's tails from the sheep barn.

Watching our (then) toddler sons handle very large shovels led me once to buy them some shovels that were a little more their size. They were under the Christmas tree one morning. Though they brought big smiles to a couple of pint-sized boys, the larger one was a little less impressed. The shovels were about 36 inches in height and were made of plastic from one end to the other. But they only cost three bucks each. Being the two little bulls in a china shop that they were then, I figured we weren't out much if—or when--they broke.

"Those things won't last a week," my husband said under his breath as the boys gleefully opened them. They immediately began to shovel the piles of wrapping paper into a corner as they ignored all other Christmas delights.

The least they could have done was start shoveling all the corn and oats off of the basement floor that had filled the insides of their small work boots as they trudged around inside the grain bins with their dad. But shoveling corn out of the house seemed less appealing.

They must have gotten that from me.

Those new Christmas shovels went right outside to scoop snow, chop ice and "comb" the dog's hair, as the dog sat patiently and let them hone their grooming skills. The shovels also helped clean out the farrowing house and went with them in the pickup as they tagged along to help clean up grain from around the stopped auger during fall harvest. Yes siree—those shovels scooped as much sand, snow, hog feed, manure and corn as four-year-olds could scoop.

It was quite a few years later when my husband and I were doing chores and saw those little plastic shovels hanging in the feed shed. They were smeared with all the things a regulation farm shovel is smeared with—feed, a little hog manure here and there, a little corn, and the edges of them were nicked and worn, just like the real thing. They looked a little worse for the wear, but they were still around, and 100 percent intact. It was amazing.

Who knew something so cheap would be around so long? I just hope my husband didn't think that same thing of me.

A little later on they graduated to an actual metal sand shovel, also made for very small children. They received the same treatment, getting a workout in the farrowing house, feed shed, and in the garage and around the house--scooping snow and ice. They passed a lot of time for two young farm boys who were always looking for something to do.

Today they hang on the wall in the basement, serving as reminders of a time when life was much simpler for them—when they were just venturing out and learning what it meant to work around the farm. And as in Shel Silverstein's story of "The Giving Tree," our boys grew up and left them behind to pursue the more grown-up world of farming.

If only those little shovels could talk. I really miss those days.

WHAT THE FARM WIFE IS THANKFUL FOR

L et's face it. There are a lot of things in which a farmer's wife can be knee-deep. It may be cooking, book work, laundry, children, canning and the garden, debt, livestock dung, or the fertilizer she hears over the fence as her husband and neighbors exchange stories.

But as we wallow in all of this knee-deep-ness, we're reminded that once a year isn't nearly often enough to realize that we have it pretty good compared to many in our world. Gratitude comes in many forms. Here is the farm wife's top 10 list:

1. Carpet made of corn. Not only does it help her bottom line as a producer, but with all the corn she vacuums out of it, she can sell it and take that dream vacation she never got because there's too much work to do on the farm. She may need to supplement with the corn she harvests out of shoes, pockets, tractors and the washer and dryer when commodity prices are low.

2. Scotch-Guard. For the farm wife, scotch-guard is a must; and sometimes she doesn't even need the "guard" part as much as the "scotch" as she works tirelessly to keep it clean out here on the prairie. She never knows who or what will show up on it.

3. Potato chip cylinder containers. For the farm mom who needs to come up with something that will double as a silo

on her young children's toy farm, they're irreplaceable. It's one of her first experiences in thinking like her husband, and attempting to solve farm problems.

4. Sewing machines. Mending carries with it a kind of love-hate relationship, but it does seem to keep the relationship going between the farmer and his checkbook. It's part of her contribution to successful farm cash flow. Michelangelo has nothing over the farm wife who mends blue jeans. Over time, they become pieces of art as well, except they end up in the trash barrel eventually, instead of the Smithsonian. Oh, the injustice.

5. Casseroles. The farm wife must find something that can be kept warm in the oven until her hungry crew deems it no longer useful to be outside. If it's late enough, they may also deem it not useful to come in, finding that cacti have more hydration than their supper, which has been warming in the oven since baling season started.

6. Neighbors. Whether it's an unexpected livestock round-up or she's stuck in the mud, her neighbors are always ready to help. And usually, all it costs is a 12-pack of some kind of hop-filled beverage. Her husband may need some, too, when she tells him the story.

7. Dark towels. Hands get washed in a hurry sometimes as the farm family races from one filthy, greasy project to another. Only a farm wife can truly appreciate the value of a dark towel by the sink. There are some things she just doesn't need to see.

8. Garden hoses. While they make her life easier in many ways, it especially helps her to be able to bend dried manure-covered jeans to get them into the washing machine, instead of having to wrestle them in.

9. Large-capacity washing machines. Lambing and calving season?? Enough said. Yeesh.

10. Her life on the farm. The farm wife knows she's helping to give her children a childhood that not everyone gets to experience. The farm is a teacher with a barn, and the lessons learned on the land can't be learned from textbooks.

Finally, the farm wife is thankful for the time she gets to spend with her husband. Often times it's spent working together because free time is at a premium. Though it's not necessarily romantic, she understands that he's singlehandedly keeping 155 people in food every year. And she can't think of anything she'd rather be knee-deep in doing.

WHEN DREAMS MEET REALITY

It happened to us a few years ago. Well, mostly, it happened to my husband, but it involved all the rest of us who have carried both his last name and many a feed pail in the name of pegging away at something that was larger than the one-ton lady at the circus freak show.

It began when we discovered our neighbors were going to sell their acreage and some farm land surrounding it. Our children were of the age that they were going to be facing the world on their own soon, and since they would be farming with us, we thought it would be a nice place for them to live and a smart investment.

My husband had always dreamed of owning and farming a piece of land that connected to the grass that surrounds his house. He had farmed land that surrounded our own acreage for many years. Although it was fun, the crop belonged to the farmer for whom he worked.

But it fanned a spark that had always been smoldering.

We met with the family and our bankers, bid on the acreage and some of the farm land, and soon found ourselves signing transfer-of-ownership papers, and a hefty bank note.

I prayed to get outside the door of the bank before I revisited my lunch.

Wow.

It was the start of antacids as part of my regular diet. But it was the start of a dream that took on a life of its own for my husband.

His hard work and frugalness had put him into a position to capitalize on his dream when it presented itself. His face could hardly hold his smile.

Planting a corn crop on land that had our names on it changed the meaning of planting season for my husband. When he was ready to plant on that land, he called and asked if I wanted to come over and ride with him. It was exciting. I had never owned farm land, either.

He set the planter down, checked the monitors, adjusted whatever was necessary, and set out down the edge of the field, nearly giddy. He stopped now and then, got out of the tractor, found his pliers and examined the seed depth and population. He drove along watching the planter, then looked ahead and occasionally into my eyes saying, "This is so cool."

I agreed with him whole-heartedly, but didn't truly understand until then—and until that growing season, just how connected a farmer is to the land. To me, the corn meant income for our family. To him it was a chance to live the life he'd always wanted to live; to pass the same dream on to our children, and hopefully—with good decisions and some luck—pass on opportunity and land to them someday after we are gone.

He'd been dreaming of planting that corn since he used to sit in class at school and create drawings of hog houses instead of listening to his teachers. He had put in years of planning already, and he wasn't even out of school yet.

Dreams are powerful, and if staying power and elbow grease are the keys to realizing them, they can produce remarkable results. These days when my husband leaves the yard with a tractor and his dreams attached to it in the spring—in whatever implement form those dreams take—I know he's as content as a farmer can be. The whole growing season is ahead, and anything can happen when Mother Nature is in charge.

Each year he hopes there will be enough corn in the bin to keep going, and enough to put onto a ship headed for China with a U.S. flag attached to it. After all, some of that corn could be his, and he knows that agriculture is even bigger than his own dreams.

It's part of a well-orchestrated gamble every year. And it all started with a corn field.

And a dream.

HARVESTING THE MEMORIES

A little bit of nostalgia left our farm today.
I thought those same words when our daughter left for college, only we knew we would see her again on breaks and over the holidays. This nostalgia was leaving, never to return.

It was an old John Deere "95" diesel hydrostatic combine.

It was the first combine we ever owned—a purchase we made from my brother back in the day. It was one more step forward on my husband's life-long dream of farming. As we visited with my brother about it in the days before the combine came to live with us, he told us, "She's a good ole' combine." And she was.

Our children were toddlers when we first met this combine. They were so little that they couldn't get up the fold-down steps without help. They thought it was the best combine—because it was the one their dad used.

What it really was, was the best of times.

It's the machine that harvested crops from our first field—three rows at a time--and where my husband dreamed of what else could be. And it's where our children first learned to love the harvest as much as their dad did.

A man once asked my husband what he used for a combine. When he said he used a John Deere "95" the man thought he meant a "9500."

"Nope," my husband said. "....a 95."

The man seemed a little surprised that someone would be using a dinosaur like that, but I'll bet he hadn't looked in our machine shed before he asked that question. If he had, he would have seen an Allis Chalmers "190." It showed that we were young farmers trying to get started, and buying what we could afford at the time. It was also fun to drive.

A metal collector once offered my husband some money in exchange for the soul of the combine—but he couldn't let it go. It just wasn't time yet.

In the years that have passed, we've expanded, and all of our children grew up to be involved in agriculture. The "95" was demoted to the grove. We bought newer machinery, and in "Puff the Magic Dragon" style, the older our children became, the less that combine was part of their lives. I mowed around it for years and wished I didn't have to. After all, it wasn't doing us any good anymore.

Then today, two men from Audubon County came to take it home with them to use it to combine oats. Money was exchanged and the combine was loaded up on the trailer behind their semi. All that was left were the farewells. The combine waited patiently above us, looking down on the farm it called home and on the people who took a chance on it all those years ago. It was going to a new home where it would be used again—it would have a purpose. It would be happy again. And there was bittersweet joy in that.

Finally, slowly, the combine left the yard. I watched until the gravel road dust made it impossible to see it anymore. It was a good run, and all I had to do was look around to see what it helped us accomplish. It was a long time ago, but it was still part of our farm story.

Miley Cyrus sang a song that echoes true for so many things—it really isn't the destination, "...it's the climb." And for our family, that climb was as long and difficult as it was wonderful, from a rear-view mirror perspective.

That combine played an important role in our climb. There was time spent together in the cab with a hopeful husband and father...and three future farmers...his next dream.

She was a good ole' combine.

DRAFTING A RECORD

The day was warm and humid as people side-stepped water puddles.

Horse whinnies graced the air occasionally and mule teams brayed as they stood proudly beside their counterparts in U.S. ag history, remembering, and waiting their turn.

There was something in the air. Excitement. Buzzing. More people than usual. Patience. Anticipation. Waiting.

A world record attempt was to be made at the 2016 Albert City Threshermen and Collector's Show as organizers worked tirelessly to bring as many draft horses onto the grounds as possible in order to pull it all off. They would try to break the 2015 Guinness world record of 84 draft horses plowing simultaneously. They wanted 100 horses to get it done.

They got 120 of them.

With five inches of rain the day before the weekend event began, conditions were not ideal. But as the saying goes in the theatre business, 'the show must go on.'

And that it did.

A couple thousand people of every age flocked to the show's west field to be witness to a world record attempt. They were looking up often because the sky was pregnant with gray clouds, and they were already walking in the mud. But they didn't seem to care. The horses waited for the official time. And so did they.

As the people gathered along the sidelines of a tract of land that was prepared for such an event, the draft horses were gathering around, too, leading small plows and their drivers to the place where they would once again try to make history. But the horses wouldn't know even if they did.

Soon came the singing of the National Anthem...followed by the rain.

But the people stayed.

The horse teams, drivers and plows were at the starting line and waiting patiently, like statues. And when the time was right, they started out, slowly but surely. It was a sight to see.

The horses trotted along gently. Steadily. Quietly. Gracefully. Methodically.

The scene was nothing short of nostalgic. The horses were focused, and it was like stepping back to a time when life was, in some ways, much more difficult--and in other ways, much simpler. It was quiet as the horses came over the hill and past us, with just the sounds of chains, reins and harnesses rattling. It was surreal.

You could hear steel wheels squeaking here and there. And rain falling. And bystanders cheering them on quietly. "They're going to do it ... " I heard someone say.

I thought about the way America was built—and much of it was done on dirt and with horses as people began to homestead this land in those original "every-man-for-himself" days. I have to say that, not being a horse person at heart, I gave considerable thought to the fact that my grandfather and father saw some of this action before 'horsepower' became a word associated with tractors.

Seeing this, I wondered how farming has continued throughout so many generations with the unrelenting hard labor it entailed then. Who would want to work that hard? The truth is, that life became part of who they were—and it happens that way still today.

Those draft horses came over the hill with the grace and style of 120 gifted ballerinas.

People said, "It was worth standing in the rain to see."

And it was.

World record or not, the horses went back to the barn that night as always, not even knowing how special they are to an era of people who remember... or what they taught to an era of people who don't.

THE COST OF CHRISTMAS

Sometimes I don't know which phrase is more daunting: "I sold hogs for tomorrow." Or "The holidays are coming."

Both of those phrases can cause break-ups of relationships between relatives if the event is handled improperly, and both can result in seeking out the secret brandy bottle hidden in the chicken coop and saved for sharpening those coping skills—or maybe even for eliminating the need for them altogether.

Let's face it. When the holidays arrive there are many stressors that come with them, and affording the celebration ranks as high as General Patton did in his day.

Farm families have known for generations that some years they "have" and some years they "have not." It's no secret, and sometimes I wonder how many times farm people have nipped at the hidden brandy bottle over the years before deciding they wanted to live like that.

Growing up, we had no idea what Mom and Dad spent on us each year at Christmas. As children, all seven of us kids received three things—something we needed, something we wanted, and a surprise. While it was a sensible plan for spending, it had to have been quite a burden just doing the shopping, let alone paying for it and getting everything wrapped for Christmas morning.

But Christmas isn't just about financing and opening the gifts, of course. To my father—a farmer and a great problem-solver, Christmas fun sometimes included some mystery. One year our youngest brother got a special gift for Christmas, but it was the way in which it was given that made that Christmas so memorable that year.

He opened a box that was under the tree with his name on it, and the box held a paper that gave him instructions on where to go in the house or on the farm to find another box with his name on it. He went there and found another box with instructions--- and he did this seven times. We followed him around the farm that cold morning like common street gang members as he (and we) went from place to place in search of what was waiting for him. The final box contained a clue that led us to an empty grain bin--- where our brother's brand new bike awaited him, fully assembled.

Dad grew up with skimpy Christmas mornings as a kid in the 1930s and 40s. That morning had to be fun for him. On the other hand, my brother was exhausted--appearing like he'd just returned from the Serengeti after hunting down the evening meal's main course.

The bike was costly, I'm sure, but we all still remember that Christmas morning.

When the hog market tanked in 1998, my husband and I had more hogs here than at any other time in our production history, and less money than we had ever had as well. What were we going to do for Christmas for our three young children who were beginning to wonder about the validity of this so-called 'Santa Claus'? If Santa was scanty our cover would be blown because they all knew things were tough on the farm. We couldn't even afford the tissues we needed to cry about it that year.

Christmas arrived and brought them a few small things....along with new bikes for each of them, which they did need and want. Our cover was not blown and Santa Claus remained a real person in their minds and hearts. We couldn't afford it—even though the bikes were not expensive ones, but it was worth it to keep Santa Claus in our Christmas celebration for another year. At least we had that great memory from such an awful year on the farm.

We managed to find the money somehow.

Love is expensive, as they say. Sometimes the cost of Christmas is worth the pain.

THE GRAIN CART OPERATOR

One harvest season when we found ourselves a little short of help, my husband approached me to see if I would drive the grain cart, which I had never done before.

I agreed to the job, thinking, "How hard can it be?" After all, our sons learned the job when they were in the fourth grade. My sister who has lived in town all of her adult life caught grain for my brother once only a few harvest seasons ago—and the only other time I remember her driving a tractor was when she told Mom to go to (you know where) under her breath once.

She wasn't counting on Mom hearing her, of course, so she sent my sister out to Dad and told him to give her something to do. Dad made her paint the gas barrel and drag the yard with the old Ford tractor in exchange for her ill-timed and louder-than-planned commentary and analysis.

(How do mothers hear things like that, and not our outright pleas for clothes like all the cool kids wear?)

I have ridden with the guys before during harvest and have always been graciously thankful that I was not the one responsible for keeping the tractor just inches from the bean head as they rolled together through the field. And yet I thought that if our fourth grade sons could pick up on it, I should be able to do it, too.

The first day I packed up all the necessities—my lunch, some toilet paper and my sports bra to keep everything in place during those hurried trips back to the combine after a load dump.

A few lessons on speed and how many rows to be over, and I was flying solo in no time. I thought it was a pretty good gig and wondered why no one ever wants that job.

The learning curve appeared when we got into a wet hole and the tractor became bogged down. As we worked briefly to free ourselves from the quagmire, someone asked me, "Is your differential on?"

My eyes were spinning like those of long-ago cartoon characters that had just been coldcocked. I couldn't find it on the 'Mission Control' panel in the tractor and I couldn't find it via my husband's instructions on the radio, so another guy stepped in and found it for me.

If my husband would have told me it looks like the T.V. pictures of shingles that people get, I would have spotted it right away.

A simple communication issue.

One of the corn fields we got into was hilly. And I mean hilly.

I went over the first big hill with the tractor and grain cart and felt like I was scaling the first climb of a roller coaster. The sign at the top of the coaster at Arnolds Park says, "The Point of No Return." I saw that sign in my mind as I neared the summit and prayed there was land on the other side. I felt a little like the great explorers must have felt---Christopher Columbus and Yukon Cornelius.

It felt like we were gleaning the Matterhorn, and I thought that if I heard yodeling or spotted the Von Trapp family over the next hill, I was going to need some of that paper on a roll that I referred to earlier.

My husband asked me to top off a truck one day, which I did. I overloaded it by 8,000 pounds according to the scale at the elevator. (I overloaded it by 18,000 pounds if you don't count the extra 10,000 pounds they give farm trucks temporarily for farm-to-market hauling.)

I guess farm wives can add elevator scales to the list of scales that rat us out and laugh at us secretly.

A high school guy working for us said incredulously of the overload, "That's impressive."

My husband had another word for it.

The good news is that after my experience this fall, I won't have to do toning exercises on my left thigh for months after all that standing on the clutch while loading the trucks.

Fourth grade was a long time ago. Imagine how sleek my thighs would be by now.

THE HAPPIEST PLACE

This past year as Christmas came and went, I thought about how our Christmas celebrations have changed over the years, and of the places I have been on Christmas Eve.

As I have said before, if you marry a farmer, you can assume that any forthcoming children will be born primarily during winter months, lest there is a crop to plant or harvest, or hay to get cut and baled before the rain comes.

Our daughter, our oldest child, came to us in early December, and had her first Christmas just days into her life. From her demeanor that first Christmas, it became apparent that holidays weren't her thing. She told us in no uncertain words...well, in no words...that our focus should be on our own baby, and maybe not so much the one Mary and Joseph had all those years ago. Still, we celebrated both amazing babies.

Fast-forward a year and a few months when I found myself in the doctor's office again on a prenatal visit. It was exciting to give our daughter a sibling—but our doctor had a surprise.

He frowned as he measured me on my second prenatal visit, and I only slightly panicked. After all, I had frowned many times over the years myself taking my measurements.

He said there could be more than one in there, and a July sonogram told just that story.

I remember well the drive home. My husband was silent all the way, imagining the financial impact. I was aghast with much

more practical thoughts like, "Oh Lord, I have to push TWO babies out.", and thinking that once again, I was back to being a
pregnancy novice.

When we got to my in-laws' home to pick up our daughter, we
gave them the first news of twins. My mother-in-law said very factually what we were all thinking. "Well, I'll be damned."

She just laid it right out there. And she said it twice—she was
already getting the hang of this twin thing.

Time marched on and after six weeks of total bed rest and two
sieges of nauseating labor-stopping medications in as many months,
our sons decided to arrive three weeks early—just four days before
Christmas. After a whole day of Houdini-ism, they were taking too
long to break out—so the doctors decided to go in after them.

It seemed ironic to me that the longest day of my life was on
the shortest day of the calendar year.

The next day as our two brand new sons were in their isolettes
in my room, I remembered sitting on the edge of my bed looking at them, and being aghast once again with recurring thoughts
such as, "How am I going to take care of two babies?" I knew already how all-consuming one baby was to care for; now we had two
at the same time, plus a two-year old.

A neighbor had earlier sensed my fears as an expectant mother
of twins. She told me, "You know honey, one baby takes all of your
time. Two aren't going to take any more of it."

Somehow, those words really helped, and have stuck with me
all these years.

That Christmas Eve I found myself alone in a hospital room in
a town 45 minutes away from our home, waiting for my husband to
arrive. I was overcome with gratefulness for people who work on
Christmas Eve, caring for others instead of being home with their
own families.

Luckily, there was room for us at the inn that Christmas, disguised as a hospital, when time came for us to bring forth our

children. And being hog farmers, there truly was a chance that my husband could arrive smelling like a stable on our first Christmas with three children.

We all came home together, healthy, on Christmas Day. Talk about some kind of Christmas gift.

And so—the happiest place I ever was on a Christmas Eve was in an unfamiliar hospital room in a strange town after a long pregnancy journey, knowing no one, but getting to know our new family members. It was very Mary-and-Joseph-like, except without donkey slobber just a few feet away.

By the looks of things, there would be plenty of baby slobber to make up for it in the months ahead of us.

CHILLIN' ON LIFE

We learn about life from so many people who come into and out of our lives. Those people can teach us to appreciate so many things—or they can come as lessons for us.

That can be good or bad, depending on how you look at it. Here's a good example: a kid once wrote an answer to the question, "How would you make marriage work?" His answer was, "... tell your wife she looks pretty even if she looks like a dump truck."

I'd like to meet that kid.

Or how about the kid who, on a rainy day, told his mother he wasn't afraid of the lightning because it meant God was taking his picture?

It's all in how you look at it. Perspective. We complicate things so much as adults.

Every new year we resolve to be better, do better, try harder and reach goals that we didn't accomplish in the last year. A friend of mine once excitedly told me about her upcoming trip to California. In the same conversation, I excitedly told her of our new counter-height bathroom sinks and high toilets that were going into our bathrooms in our home.

It was our perspectives on happiness, though I'm pretty sure she thought I should get a life.

From the time our daughter was little, I would sit at the edge of her bed at night and talk to her about all kinds of things. I started out close beside her because she wasn't all that big in those very early years. But over time I noticed that I was sitting back a little further as we talked. She was growing up, and I could either love it or fight it. I knew I would never win that fight, so I chose to love it, albeit, with sadness in my heart sometimes as I left her room.

The year she was married, the path to the altar was a rocky one at best because of all the issues that hovered over the process. My father-in-law became ill and was hospitalized six weeks before the wedding. Plans went on, clouded by the fact that he was gravely ill. Family members took turns sitting by his hospital bed day and night, waiting for what would eventually come. And yet, the wedding plans went on.

One evening as we waited in his hospital room, our daughter was going over her wedding planning notes, when she began to wipe tears away. She said, "It's no fun planning my wedding from Grandpa's hospital room." It was wedding planning from her perspective.

That very sweet man went to heaven just one week before her wedding. I felt sorrow for so many people, but especially for my husband and our daughter. For my husband, he would bury his father and give away his only daughter all in the same week. For our daughter, the happiest day of her life was clouded by such a rough week, and the memory of another man whom she loved so much. Her wedding day was bittersweet, and it gave us all a new perspective on the fragility and the enormity of this life.

For a few days, we worked on wedding plans and funeral plans simultaneously, and we had to give thought to which event we were planning.

Last Mother's Day I was putting together a message to send to a friend who had lost her baby just weeks before she was to be born. I knew it would mean something to her that someone remembered her child, and the emotional pain that she herself has felt every day since then. After all, she is still a mother—even if the mother of an angel.

At the same time I was about to send it, I received a text from one of my sons—from a tractor in the field miles from here, wishing me a happy Mother's Day. I had a new awakening in that moment of the very special way in which I had been blessed. He got to grow up and was able to send me a Mother's Day message. Because of the project at hand, my heart thought about mothers everywhere who have never experienced that. His text message was enough.

Life is mostly what we make it—even if we need to turn it upside down from time to time and see it in a new perspective.

PLANTING THAT SEED

Springtime on the farm. It should give us visions of tulips blooming and blowing in the breeze, fresh air, clothes drying on the line, children playing in the yard and tractors humming in fields in the distance as they work ground and plant the crops.

What it often does show us is ankle-deep mud, a mud room that suggests people might want to wipe their feet before they go outside, four-legged mothers and babies in the barn that need our attention, ferociously-stinky barn clothes, and the sound of metal-on-metal pounding and profanities coming from the machine shed as equipment is readied for spring planting.

We begin to see things we haven't seen in a long time....... sunlight past 5 p.m., temperatures that begin without a "minus" sign, babies in the barns, insulated coveralls hanging on basement hooks instead of on people, and pickup trucks parked in groups in front of the shop as farmers gather together to collaborate and compare stories.

Farmers have many business partners. A dream is taken to the banker, who can single-handedly determine if the farmer should proceed with it or put together a resume.

Once the dream is approved by the money gods, then there are many others to place on the team every year—including seed and chemical sales people, agronomists, equipment/implement dealers, repair shops, tire shops, auto parts stores, steel salespeople, livestock sales people, livestock sale barn managers, veterinarians, building companies, fuel delivery people, feed supply dealers and of course, the tax preparer.

But even with all the people it takes to help a farmer do what he/she does every year, there is one partner who goes almost unnoticed by most. That partner is as important as the dream is, yet He is content to remain a silent partner—providing the most basic necessities a farmer needs to give back from the earth.

A farmer can only do "so much" to grow a crop. But if the rains never came and there was no soil in which to plant a crop and no sunshine to make plants grow, the farmer's hands would be tied.

This spring we had a couple of urban youth come out to our farm to bottle feed some lambs. What they experienced was new life--a baby lamb being born—with no edits.

Their hands covered their eyes now and then as they watched, and comments of, "Ouch....." and "...that must hurt..." along with their saucer-like eyes were all it took to remember that new life—even out in the barn—is always miraculous, no matter how old you are, and no matter how many times you've seen it.

God uses farmers—less than two percent of His people—to do that work of His on earth. God made the whole world dependent upon that two percent of the population to give them all they need to live—food, fuel and fiber.

The farmer is one who works directly with God to make a living each year. He has to.

In that comparatively smaller way, a farmer understands the pressures God faces. The world depends on the farmer to sustain life, and the farmer depends on God for the same thing.

To plant a seed is to have hope. And to harvest it, well, is nothing short of a miracle.

CALLING IT A HARVEST

You have to admit that there's a certain excitement that comes with the harvest.

To non-farm people, it's a mysterious time of year when slow-moving farm equipment comes out of sheds and complicates traffic routes, and fields are buzz-cut with combines.

The young urban grandson of a friend of mine commented on a corn field they drove past on their way to school, saying, "I'm sure glad that field got mowed."

Now that the harvest has finished up, it brings a sense of relief, even though it brought just as much excitement at the beginning of that long and arduous task.

For the farm wife, who often is called to be a farmer herself by way of the help she lends to the operation in driving tractors or trucks for harvest or handling the livestock chores while everyone else is in the field--then feeding everyone wherever they are working—it's especially gratifying to be done with that job. After all, she does triple duty during that time of year.

She handles her job in town and takes care of the home, yard and family all year long. But when the harvest arrives, she adds that to her list of things to get done as well, in whatever form that takes. I used to joke about leaving my job in town at the end of the work day, then coming home to the farm and starting in on the next eight hours of work.

People laughed when I said that, but they didn't know I was telling the truth.

The first year I commanded the grain cart I was amazed at the simple beauty of that time of year. I saw pheasants, rabbits and deer come out of the corn fields, beautiful sunrises and sunsets, breathtaking silhouette pictures to keep in my mind as harvesting equipment worked underneath a fire-colored sky as dusk set in.

I couldn't help but think of the song as I gazed out across the field of ripened soybeans: "*Oh beautiful, for spacious skies, for amber waves of grain...*" When the sun worked its way down each evening, the fields (known in that song as the 'fruited plains') were beyond description. No camera could do it justice.

The last field we harvested was on a sunny afternoon. I turned the tractor and grain cart around at the end of the rows and listened to The Eagles croon their song, "Lyin' Eyes." I was going to be just a little sorry when all of this work was over because at harvest time, people are at their best. Dreams for the next year are made, people are joking around with each other on two-way radios to pass the time, critical information is shared, people work together for a common cause, they stop at night to eat a hot meal together under a setting sun, reconnecting with family and farm associates, and getting a much-needed break from the monotony.

The beauty of the harvest and of the countryside that time of year makes the ending of fall all the more bittersweet. And yet, when the dryer bin fans are whirring loudly in the yard, the windows have all been washed on the house, the combine and machinery is washed up and put away, elevator scale tickets have all been located, the garden has been preserved and tilled up, the lawn has been mowed for the last time this year, the leaves have all been gathered, and the last of the clothes have been dried on the clothes line for the year, the farm family knows they get a little respite from the rat race.

That is, until they remember that tax preparation time is coming...and that they need to prepare for winter lambing and calving...and buy seed for next year....and plan fields, machinery purchases and farrowing schedules.

They know that when the spring rush arrives once again, they'll probably be seeing more rats' hind ends, because few are the years when they're actually out in front of that race.

Stupid rats, anyway.

STUMBLING UPON SUCCESS

While the Clay County Fair in Spencer has a lot of reasons to boast success, there are also a lot of reasons why it should have been a colossal flop from its very beginning.

The fact that is has been anything but a flop is a testament to the men and women who, especially in 1917 and 1918, dared to roll up their sleeves to see that dream of a new and improved county fair come to life. The truth is, if you want it bad enough, you have to get other people on board with you, and you have to be willing to do the work.

Even if you are the Clay County Fair.

Those dreamers in 1917 and 1918 were just coming off of World War I. But they began the process of creating a new venue that would give the people in the Spencer and surrounding area a place to gather, socialize, shop, eat, show their livestock, be entertained and get away from all the pressures of daily living—which is amazing to me, given the financial status of most people at that time. Some must have haughtily thought they were only dream chasers.

But 100 years, millions of people and hundreds of thousands of corn dogs and nutty bars later, they could not have been more wrong.

The success of the Clay County Fair has always baffled me. It comes at a time of year when rural people are often beginning to harvest, children are back to school, the state fair has been finished for weeks and the weather is as unpredictable as a wandering gypsy fortune teller.

And yet, it has served as an official end to summer no matter what goes on--in scorching heat and in drenching rains. Even a terrorist attack on the United States on September 11, 2001 did not stop the fair. It dampened and sobered-up the spirit, but it did not ravage the core purpose of a county fair. It gave us a place to grieve together as one people.

Early on in that crisis, the fair served mostly as a distraction from the grim realities of life—and the massive loss of it. The fallout would eventually change the world—and each of us.

The fact that the people of 1918 envisioned a grandstand at all was futuristic thinking, and the idea that a new grandstand would appear in 1931 is nothing short of miraculous.

That same year, downtown Spencer had been destroyed with the careless flick of a lit firecracker into a barrel at a corner drug store over the Fourth of July. But once again, the Clay County Fair provided a distraction and gave people something else to focus on besides the grueling mission of rebuilding. They came together to accomplish two big tasks during the stark days of the Great Depression. It's hard to imagine that kind of dedication to a county fair.

People have been married on the fairgrounds and had their wedding vows renewed there. On those occasions, they are standing on holy ground—the same ground to which they would someday bring their families.

I wonder what the Clay County Fair Association of 1917 would think if they saw the fair today. Manager Jeremy Parsons has led this epic wonder into its centennial year and says, "A lot can be accomplished when you don't care who gets the credit."

That is undeniably true in any arena of life in which we find ourselves.

Parsons also said, just before the centennial fair started: "It's like my friend used to say—'Now we just unlock the door, turn on the lights and hope somebody shows up.' "

Well, they *have* shown up—and in huge numbers, and under the best and worst of circumstances in the country and in their personal lives. For some, it simply cannot be missed.

I think the dream-based fair association of 1917 would be proud of this fair that was always meant to be successful, but never should have been.

But then, no one person ever really got the credit for the dream ... or the work.

And so it goes for a county fair that worked hard to stumble upon wild success.

OF PIGS AND BEAUTY

It was a call I had received a while ago that got me thinking. When I answered the phone there was a woman from our local extension office on the other end of the line. She asked if I would be interested in doing the announcing for the swine show at our county fair. Always up for a fun challenge, I accepted her invitation.

And that's where it all headed south.

She said, "Oh good—thank you. We thought you would be a good person to do the swine show."

It was like telling me I had a face for radio ... which I do, actually.

If I were a man, I would probably not even remember that she said that. But I'm not a man, and even if she had made that statement 15 years ago on the 23rd of May at 10:36 a.m., I would still remember it.

But I wouldn't be able to tell you how much rain we had that spring or how much rain may have fallen on that particular day. Now that would be something a man could tell you.

It got me thinking about true beauty and how it relates to life on the farm.

Even as our 2016 crop became "old crop" as soon as the new year began—and before the new crop was even planted--I was thinking of how fleeting time is, and how quickly something new can become 'yesterday's news.'

This year as I emceed that swine show, I noticed on the program for the first time that there were lots of gilts, but no sows. There have never been sows there, I suspect, but I was laughing to myself about the irony in that as I thought about how that played out in human form.

Most women who have never had children can schlep around in sleek clothing and look like a million bucks with hardly any effort, it seems. Once she has carried a child in her stretched-out tummy for nine months, she can try doing that, but her body at that point is made for other things—like feeding the baby it just carried.

It's glorious to do, but perhaps not glamorous in a style show.

In pig reality, I would be the equivalent of a sow, since I have had offspring—even two at a time—my own small litter. And I know now that the county fair does not allow for sows to parade around in front of a group of salivating bacon hoarders. Once she has little ones, a pig is no longer eligible for a beauty contest.

Oh, the injustice of it all, and the irony in that reasoning. If a judge could pick out a sow that still looked great after four or five litters, now that would really be something special.

I once sat with a friend of mine through a 4H and FFA fair swine show where our children were exhibiting. As the judge did what judges do, he made his selections for the top ones, and began to tell the crowd of parents and other onlookers about his top choice. He chose a particular pig because of its "prominent, muscly, round back end."

My friend leaned over to me and said quietly, "...so he's saying it's *good* to have a large, round behind?" She then pointed to herself and laughed, as we both did. I felt like I fit into that category as well.

Our children are in their mid- and late-20s, and I'm afraid I've nearly used up my 'baby fat' excuse time.

Poor, persecuted pig-bearing porcines. I understand their beauty plight. I'm also an inch shorter than I used to be.

I wonder if that helps give me a "...prominent, round, muscly back end?"

I'll be expecting that grand champion ribbon at next year's swine show.

WHAT'S IN A NAME?

I f you come from a family with two or three children or more, I know you have experienced it.

My older sister and I are 15 months apart. Aside from being two grades apart in school due to the times of year that we were born, teachers often got us mixed up. It was okay – our mother did that all the time. Some days she would go down the whole list of kids before she stopped at the right name. She was a very busy mother and had to have felt like the Old Woman Who Lived in a Shoe.

Being called by name was something I never thought anything of until my husband and I had twins.

Our boys grew up with people not being able to tell them apart. Of course, we can tell them apart easily, but we're around them all the time. The amazing thing was that when they were born, we truly could not tell one from the other, but their sister (two years their elder) knew right out of the chute who was whom. I guess two-year-olds don't know that twins often look the same, and so to her, they were just her two brothers who were born on the same day.

It used to amaze me ... and even intimidate me just a little, that she could out-I.D. me.

We devised a plan to ensure that the same name went to the same baby and wrote it down so we would always have it. What if one of them grew up to be an axe murderer or something? The right fingerprints would be very important; ... not that we wanted them to grow up to be axe murderers or anything......

All through school our sons answered mostly to our last name, and variations of it, because people thought at least they would get THAT right. Some kids at school had come up with a new name for them by combining both of their first names into one, thinking they had half of a chance at getting some of their name right. Some people just flat our asked, "Which one are you?" They took it well.

When our sons worked for a neighbor one summer, he said he finally had them figured out. Then they suddenly showed up to work wearing different shoes and it ruined his whole plan, and he had to start over again.

Our sons wrestled in high school—only one weight class apart. When our 215-pounder had finished wrestling, his brother came out for the heavyweight match, weighing the same as our 215-pounder. He got settled in to start the match when the referee looked down at him and said, "Weren't you just out here?"

When they were in high school they had gone to a livestock show in Des Moines to help as showmen. It turned cold while they were there and they bought pull-over jackets. A man there was operating a stand where he would sew things onto garments, and they thought they would put their names on their new jackets just for the fun of it. But it turned out to be much more than that.

Upon returning home, one of them said to me, "It was, like, the first time I heard someone (outside of the family) actually say my name to me."

Until that moment, I had never understood the true beauty that lies behind hearing the people I know and love speak my name—and to know that people know who I am whenever they see me. Our son was in high school and had not known that luxury—at least not to the extent that most of us know it. It actually made me a little sad for him.

What's in a name? Plenty, if you ask our sons, and perhaps other look-alikes.

But our boys will still grin at you if you get their names wrong, I'll becha.

A LITTLE ADVICE FOR FFA'ers

In one of his lesser romantic notions, my husband recently asked me to accompany him to Des Moines for a day-long seminar on what's coming down the pike in agriculture today.

Having married a former FFA chapter president, I guess I should not expect any more in the ways of romance. Not that much has changed, really. Thirty years ago he would ask me to accompany him to the farrowing house to help scrape it out, or to the barn to load pigs. I guess in a way I've moved up the ladder, if only slightly—coming back from a day together not smelling like something I had to scrape or power wash.

I know that for most ladies, a trip to the capital city might sound pretty inviting, but going to an all-day seminar on the outlook of American agriculture?

Please.

But for this farm wife who has navigated through a couple of serious farm crisis years, I felt like my time was better spent beside my husband, learning about all those things, too, instead of spending the day shopping.

While I didn't soak in every nugget that he did, I was very intrigued by one of the things the group did while they were there. At one point the organizer held up a book of blank pages and asked each farmer to write some kind of advice they would give to today's FFA members. The leaders of the day would then write up a summary and distribute them to various FFA chapters.

It was a stellar idea and I couldn't wait for the book to come around to us, to see what other farmers had to say to their much younger counterparts in agriculture. Here is a sampling of what we read and wrote as a group:

- "Practice having positive outcomes in your life—expectations influence outcomes."
- "Farming is a way of life (and) a business. Manage your farm like a business."
- "You miss 100 percent of the shots you don't take."
- Over the years Grandpa and Dad always expected us to know certain things about farming. This is a good thing because if you are expected to know something, you will learn it."
- "It's never too late to come back and pursue your dream."
- "Adopt new technology early."
- "Take care of the land and it will take care of you. It's a privilege to be a steward of the land. Let's be faithful stewards and pass it on to the next generation."
- "Business goes where it is invited and stays where it is served."
- "Try again next year."
- "Learn from your mistakes and improve."
- "To grow 300 bushel corn we have to think 300 bushel corn."
- "God and hard work."
- "Agriculture is the optimistic science. Ten percent of life is what happens to you. Ninety percent of life is how you deal with it."
- "Too soon old, too late smart." *(Old German saying)*
- "Treat people you do business with the way you want to be treated."
- "Farming takes everything you've got—financially, physically, emotionally and spiritually. You can manage them all by always keeping your head in the game."

Farmers are not showy people. They are hard workers who are more willing to listen to others than they are to give advice. Most don't feel qualified to give advice—after all, most farmers have had at least one bad year or made at least one bad decision.

But maybe stumbling at least once in this business gives us the right to be able to reach into the depths of our hearts and think of what we would tell someone just getting into this business that has offered us to much satisfaction—and so much pain some years.

These great words of advice came straight from the farmers' hearts and were given with hope to the next generation of American farm families. History tells us we're destined to repeat the mistakes of our forefathers if we don't learn from them. This was an outreach from today's farmers to teach your children about the importance of sustaining the land and being successful at what they do.

It takes a village to raise a child ... as well as tomorrow's farmers.

It was way better than shopping.

"RURAL" IN THE MIND'S EYE

There's an awful lot of pride out here in the nation's heartland. Part of that comes from the fact that, in order to live in the heartland, you first have to have a lot of heart; and if you have a shred of work ethic to pair it with, then you'll fit in without even being noticed. That's just the way I think rural people are.

When I think of the word "rural," it creates a lot of visual images. I think of the mailbox at the end of a farm driveway. I think of the noon-time meal of "dinner," and the evening meal of "supper." I see sweaty people stacking bales on a hay rack.

I think of a barn--and a basketball hoop in the hay mow; silos, grain bins, and a yellow school bus coming down the road at 7:15 a.m. to pick up kids who may have already been out to do their chores by then. I see row crops, a tire swing hanging from an old cottonwood tree, and semi trucks on the county fairgrounds, backed up to the show arena on livestock sale day....and 4-H and F.F.A. kids of all ages showing their animals that day with heavy hearts and even through outright tears.

Yes, the rural life is a rich and layered one, indeed.

I did a very unofficial survey recently, asking other people what the word "rural" meant to them. Their answers were better than anything I could have come up with:

- Grandparents' farms, with ponds at which to go fishing, and hearing the farm animals bellering and birds singing; neighbors pulling together to help each other out;
- Seeing God in all things that grow; rejoicing in having such a great place to raise children;
- Meeting a farmer driving an old tractor on the road (gravel flying behind it), and receiving the "official farmer's wave" of the index finger being lifted from the steering wheel;
- The different colors of the fields throughout the seasons--the black of late winter/early spring; the green of spring and summer; the harvest-gold color of fall, and the white of winter, covering the ground like a blanket and once again, letting it rest;
- One grown-up 'city kid' said she loved it when she visited her farm cousins on vacation when she was growing up because of how basic their lives were--from food, to work, to family;
- Little farming towns, large, old wooden barns; farmers who love what they do and teach the same love of the land and animals to their own children; the farmer's hat; watching beautiful sunrises and sunsets over land filled with growing crops;
- Late night suppers, close-knit relationships where neighbors are like extended family members; working hard and long hours, but having fun doing that work;
- The amazing feeling of accomplishment when finishing a field or raising livestock and knowing it will help feed America; a life that brings family and friends closer, and the special bond you have with people in small town communities; fair time and showing livestock with your friends, and missing the people from your hometown once you move away;

- Hard work; the quiet; and friends who understand what your life is like;
- Being in tune with nature; understanding the connection to the land that can't be explained, but must be felt; sitting on the front porch and hearing the crickets and watching the stars;
- Being able to walk downtown (alone) at age seven, because everyone looked out for everyone; when the 6:00 whistle blew, you knew it was time to go home to eat supper; neighborhood baseball games, church potluck dinners, and baking Christmas goodies and taking them to elderly shut-ins;
- Cattle and sheep grazing on a hill (no confinements); a big white house with chickens and a couple of cows, and kids going to the barn to swing on the big rope inside so they can land in the straw below; a garden; clothes hanging on the line;
- A strong work ethic, determination to make a better life for all the people they care about; early mornings, late nights, working together; trusting your neighbors and not expecting payment for helping them; making due; home-cooked meals enjoyed as a family (sometimes at odd hours) on a daily basis; prayers, Sunday morning church service, and supporting kids' school activities; trusting that when you help your neighbors and friends, that they will be there to help you in your hour of need also.

And so I ask you, what does "rural" mean to you?

One of my Iowa respondents concluded, "Where else but in rural America would these things happen? Thank God we were born and raised in rural Iowa."

A MOTHER'S LETTER

Dear Daughter,

In a few days you will become a mother for the first time. Maybe you will become a mother over and over again in your lifetime, but rest assured that while all of your pregnancies and babies/children will be special, there's just something about that first one.

You were that first one for me. Until you were born I couldn't possibly understand how someone so small could have such a huge impact on my life. Carrying you for nine months was one of the most profound experiences of my life. It was all so new to me, and it held lots of mystery and a certain kind of joy that nothing else in my life could come close to matching.

Finally the time came for you to be born. It was a scary time, but there you were—pink and perfect. Casting our eyes upon you in the flesh for the very first time was unbelievable. I knew you before you were born, and up until then, I had carried you every second of your life.

And now you come to these last few days before having a child of your own—a son. It will be the toughest job you'll ever love. You will have the blessing and arduous job of raising someone's husband—and you'll want to do a good job of that.

It will be hard sometimes. You will be overwhelmed now and then and you will have to make tough decisions. You will discipline with a heavy heart, and at times you may even feel like your children hate you—but your love for them will never waver. And on those days when you don't feel very glamorous or popular with your children, just remember that Adam was created in the wild, and Eve was created in a garden. You will always be beautiful.

Parenthood—like marriage--is a marathon. You'll be a mother for the rest of your life, so it's important to pace yourself. Remember, "Inch by inch, life is a cinch. Yard by yard, life is hard." Keep that saying close by; you will need it.

There is hardly a word in the English language that sounds as beautiful to a woman as the word, "Mom." I think God must have designed that word, because there is no other explainable reason that when a child somewhere out in public says or shouts, "Mom!" –every woman turns her head. THAT's how special it is to be a mother.

God has blessed you with this little boy. Take the time to talk to him, play with, teach, love, nurture and discipline him, give him the gift of saying "no" when you have to, but say "yes" whenever you can. And when he gets to be a toddler and wants to kiss you impetuously, let him do it. That time passes all too quickly, and someday you will long for those days back.

Give him purposeful work as he grows—something he can be proud of as he labors. Time is shorter than you realize---and before you know it, he'll be off to his first day of kindergarten, and you will be in a puddle of tears on the floor, wondering where your baby went. And when he goes off to college---well, you know the story; you were there yourself not that long ago. You will have shared so much together until then, and the tears will flow once again.

He will be a product of his environment—so make it a good one. The best thing you can give to your children is a healthy marriage, so stay close to each other, talk to each other, remain united in your efforts to raise your children together, and go to church as a family.

And when you face rough times in your relationship, take time to regroup; your decisions affect the happiness and well-being of your whole family—so make good communication part of every day. And when you need to get away by yourselves for a day or two in order to do that, you only have to call 1-800-GRANDPA-AND-GRANDMA. We work cheap when it comes to grandies.

Once this baby arrives, you will be different. You will be a more dimensional version of yourself, but you will also be the person God chose to care for this child of His. We will be learning, too, so please be patient with us as we learn to grandparent in a world that is so different from the world in which we raised you.

Dad and I wish you all the best as you start your new role as parents—the toughest, most rewarding job a person can ever love, this side of heaven.

With Love,
Mom

LIFE LESSONS FROM THE CORN

We see it all the time—we admire it, we drive past it, we walk in it, we eat it, we feed it to our livestock and pets, we hear it, we pop it, we haul it, we heat our feet and our homes with it, we fuel our cars with it, and we can even wear it.

Corn is all around us, standing there like some kind of humble, work-a-day peasant, virtually clueless as to its importance in our lives. But as it stands there so quietly in the sun and wind, it's teaching us all about life. Here are a few examples:

HAVE PATIENCE. Every tall corn stalk begins as a tiny seed. Whatever we're waiting for, it will happen in time.

PUT DOWN ROOTS. A corn stalk can't even think about growing into prosperity unless it shoots out roots to give it strength to stand. Those who have walked before us and paved the way for us are our roots in agriculture. We must remember them and learn from their successes and mistakes, and then we must shoot—and be--the roots for the next generation. Make them strong roots. Life will not always be kind.

FERTILIZER IS A MUST. No person grows into a healthy adult on their own merit. It takes the help, tolerance and encouragement of parents and an entire community to grow a child into a well-rounded adult. Praise and discipline must both be in the sprayer tank for the fertilizer that has the optimum post-emergence performance.

CULTIVATE, CULTIVATE, CULTIVATE. We are all tempted from time to time to do things we shouldn't do. Sometimes we are stronger than the temptation, and sometimes not. Corn teaches us that we need to remove bad influences from our lives in order to grow strong.

YELLOW IS NICE. The color of corn is yellow and bright. Whatever your mood as you go through life, be yellow. Everyone likes a person who shows their sunny side.

HUSKS ARE IMPORTANT. Corn husks protect the growing ear and hold in moisture. Choose the right people to be the 'husks' in your life—ones who will protect you and give you life in all of its forms. And when the time is right, pull back the 'husks' to reveal your brightness on the inside and on the outside.

TIME TAKES ITS TOLL. As corn grows, the ear eventually droops, the stalk becomes shorter and husks change from green to a yellowish-brown color. It reaches full maturity. Still, the stalk continues to stand and do the job it was meant to do regardless of what Mother Nature doles out. It can be battered and worn, but the corn stalk knows it has a job to do, and does it until the very end.

BE VERSATILE. Be willing to mix with other people, hear new ideas and try new things. It makes us better, more valuable people if we open ourselves to the value that others can bring.

HAVE A PURPOSE. A corn stalk has one purpose—to grow an ear of corn. But that one purpose affects so many other parts of life. Spend your life accomplishing your purpose, even if your growing season isn't as long as you had hoped. You never know who you are inspiring.

BLACK LAYERING ISN'T ALWAYS GOOD. While it's good in the life cycle of a corn plant, just remember to wash it off before coming to the supper table.

BLOOM WHERE YOU'RE PLANTED. The corn does this. You may not be where you want to be in life, but it's important to be your best person no matter where you have been planted.

And lastly, GIVE LIFE A WHORL.   The corn plant grows one leaf at a time out of a whorl. It will always put 100 percent of its energy into being productive, even if some leaves have been damaged along the way. Giving up is usually not an option. A corn plant is much like a farmer.

Without this kind of thinking, it would certainly be a corn-dog's life.

Err......yeah. Something like that.

THE UNUSUAL GIFT

It was no trashy gift. Well, maybe it was kind of trashy. Either way, it was a highly unusual way to express Christmas love, and peace and good will among men.

Or among husbands and wives.

One year my husband surprised me with a most unusual Christmas gift. It wasn't like the time he gave me a garbage disposal, and let me find later on that he had tucked a beautiful pair of diamond earrings inside of it.

Good save.......and a fun thing for our children to witness.

I've heard women say that if they have to plug it in, or if it can be deducted on their farmer husband's taxes, they don't really want it. I guess this means that women are not all practical, and like to be spoiled a little bit now and then.

And this is where my husband's trashy gift enters the picture.

As a farmer, he can't help but be practical in nature. It's part of who he is, and it's really one thing that is so great about almost all farmers. They like gifts that make life easier--in both giving and receiving. Really, what's not to like?

We all got up that Christmas morning--a little later than we used to get up when our children were small. Our rule back then was, "No one is up before 7 a.m." After all, with a very busy Christmas Eve elf schedule, it got late before the children could get to bed, and before Santa was able to arrive. (Even Santa was dragging pretty good by that time of night.) But back then, 7 a.m. took an eternity to arrive if you were a Schwaller kid. Not so anymore.

We gathered in the living room to have our first gander at all the gifts wrapped in beautiful paper and ribbon. That was my favorite moment with our children—seeing their faces as their eyes first fell upon all that was there for them. We got breakfast in the oven so it could be ready later, and were all making our way into the living room when I stopped at the kitchen sink to get a drink of water. It was then that I spotted it.

When I looked out the window, I could see long, red ribbons billowing from a tall pipe out in the grove. It was hooked onto something that looked like a very large barrel with a lid. As my mind was paging through ideas of what that could be out there, my husband saw me looking, smiled and said, "Hey! You're not supposed to be looking out there yet!"

Turns out, he had made me a very large trash barrel, complete with a lid that hinges open and shut, and a pipe so that the trash will burn even when the lid is closed.

It was a farm wife's dream. It seems trash barrels fill up so quickly, even when you recycle as much as you can. Burning the trash becomes a very time-consuming chore when you can only deposit a little at a time because the trash barrel is full, or because you're chasing what blew out. This one was huge, and seemed quite handy.

Many a wife -- and possibly, many a farm wife -- probably would have thought this to be less than what she had hoped for in regard to a Christmas gift. But I loved it--not only because of the fact that it would make my life (and maybe his) a little easier, but he made it himself with his two little hands--which was also pretty special. "Trashy" gift or not, it was a great one, even if my husband could deduct it from our taxes. It was part of living simply.

However, you can believe that I examined the interior like a thorough physician for a beautiful pair of diamond earrings before I ignited my first batch of trash in it.

A woman never forgets.

CARATS AND HORSEPOWER

I once became acquainted with an older woman who was here with her daughter and son-in-law. Actually, this woman was our landlady, and we had not previously met. So as we dined on some local cuisine, we sat next to each other and got to know one another.

The fact that she had worked hard in her life showed in her slow and paced walk. Yet, she was determined to get where she was going. Life lines showed on her face, tattling on years of working outside in the sun, along with all the facial lines that farming and family give us over the years—lines of worry, laughter, fear, stress and hard work.

As we visited, we got to talking about our husbands, since they both chose the same vocation--albeit, in different generations. Her husband had been gone for some time, but it was plain to see that their lives together had been happy.

Let me say next that there are men who know how to woo a woman, and then there are men who just get out there and cut right to the chase. This woman's farmer husband orchestrated both of those follies one Christmas with gangster-like success.

For all their years together, this woman worked alongside her husband, getting the farming done. She had her own tractor, and he had his. She was very proud of having her own tractor, and was possibly Iowa's original version of Gloria Steinem.

She told of one year when her husband had purchased a new tractor. The tractor was very nice, she said, but was too big for their much smaller field cultivator, which she operated. She said she couldn't believe he would buy such a big tractor for a comparatively smaller field cultivator, yet they used it because they had it.

One Christmas morning in the time following that purchase, she discovered that her gift from her husband wouldn't fit under the tree. She couldn't have imagined it, but sitting outside was a new tractor for her.

When the business world started up again following the holiday, she dialed up their insurance agent to put her new tractor on their policy. She said, "I need to get some insurance for my Christmas present."

Her agent chuckled and said, "How many carats is it?"

The woman laughed slyly and peered at me as she said boldly, "I told him, 'I'm not talking carats. I'm talking horsepower.'"

Farmers are creative people. He aced his holiday gift-giving that year by making her happy with a new tractor and increasing his popularity rating in one smooth move. He could get the work done, write it off on their taxes, take it out for a spin himself and enjoy thinking about his wife bragging of his thoughtfulness to all her friends.

He was a genius. And she was back beside him in the field.

By comparison, I was just as happy the Christmas my husband made me that hand-crafted trash barrel. *(See previous chapter.)* I didn't have to chase the burning trash that flew out of it anymore and all of the trash fit in there in one trip.

He was a genius. And I gained 10 pounds from not chasing the trash around and carrying it all out in one trip.

Apparently wife-wooing comes in many forms. But our landlady and I were both happy.

And there weren't even any carats involved.

SPLASHES, SEASHELLS AND OTHER LIFE LESSONS

For the farm family, vacation time is something that can be harder to attain than an understanding between the Kardashians and most of the free world. After all, there is work to be done—and plenty of it. All year long.

But recently we found ourselves at the shore of the Atlantic Ocean. As I stood before it for the first time, I thought about those who "farm" those waters so we can all enjoy seafood. I thought about the 1,500-plus people aboard the Titanic who died in that ocean's freezing water in April of 1912. I wondered about lost treasures that lay at the bottom, never to be found.

As I sat speechless, facing the vast and roaring ocean before me, I decided that more songs and literary masterpieces have probably been born while sitting in the mesmerizing presence of such an enormous natural resource, instead of at the back end of a farm animal having her babies...though plenty has been written about that, too.

Here is what I learned:

Be inviting; be present. The ocean does not go out to invite people to it---people just come to it because it is naturally inviting. Be the kind of person people want to come and see, and create memories. So many people in our lives look up to us and long for our attention. Always give it to them. Time is short.

Make a splash. Waves come to the shoreline--softly lapping or loudly crashing, letting us know they have arrived. Whatever you have to say or do, do it your way.

Roar when necessary. When the ocean is angry it emits a thunderous roar. When you need to, make yourself heard—however you have to do it. A mad farmer does that well.

Ocean spray is not just for cranberries. It's an unexpected pleasure. Sprinkle some unexpected joy into someone's life and watch their reaction. You will not be disappointed.

Navigate carefully. Sometimes the ocean is rough and sometimes it is calm. Life and people are that way, too. Navigate around others with care and caution. We don't always know what's ahead of us---or behind the faces they show the world.

Keep moving forward. Waves have one job—to come to shore no matter how far they have to go. In life, always keep moving forward, no matter what happens or how far away our dreams are. Always keep sight of the shore. We will get there eventually if we are patient.

Beauty comes in all forms. Waves come in all shapes and sizes, just like people. But it doesn't matter the shape or size of the wave—there is beauty in every single one, big or small.

Humility is good. Often times, small, softly-lapping waves bring as much joy as their louder, faster counterparts. Like soft waves, softly spoken words can have a significant impact.

Smooth out the shore sand. Forgiveness can be difficult to master, but just as the ocean water comes up to the shore and smooths it out, so must we be able to do that when someone wrongs us. Write peoples' transgressions in the sand, not in stone. Stones are unyielding.

Blue is beautiful. No matter how many shades of blue make up the ocean, there is beauty in every shade. When we are blue, God is holding us. Life is layered in shades of blue.

Leave something beautiful behind. The ocean waves leave gifts behind for us in beautiful, delicate seashells. Not one is the same as another, just as we are all different. As we work toward our final shoreline, always aim to leave something beautiful—our legacy--behind.

And finally, **find a way to crash.** Waves crash and return to the ocean—it's what they do. As farm people doing difficult, demanding work, it's important to "crash" (rest) when necessary, so we can return to our important work. So there we were. Resting. Recharging.

And thinking about ways the ocean reminded us about life.

CHRISTMAS SIMPLICITY

I was reading a book that my mom gave me last summer--a collection of Christmas memories from people all over the nation. Many of the stories were set around the depression era, when nobody had much to give.

And just last week when I climbed onto the elliptical to try to begin making less of myself after a harvest season sitting in the grain cart tractor, I popped in a movie that I hadn't watched in ages. It was about a family in the Blue Ridge Mountains in 1933, who also didn't have much to offer each other for Christmas except their love.

Between the book and that movie, it got me thinking about the way Christmas has changed over the years, even for my generation growing up in the '60s and '70s. Our children have not experienced Christmas the way I did while growing up, and I didn't experience Christmas the way my parents did. They were born directly after the Great Depression struck.

I remember Dad saying he got sticks for Christmas one year. A budget issue, or his behavior choices as a child that year?

You decide.

As I reflect on my childhood Christmas memories, I think about the big drawing we had in our hometown every year, the weekend before Christmas. Kids from all over town and country gathered around a hayrack sprinkled with toys at the town's main intersection.

In rural America, Santa arrives on a hayrack.

All kids received a small paper bag that held some fruit, a pack of gum or a small candy bar, and a candy cane. The bag had a number on it. If the people on the hayrack drew the number that was on your bag, you won the prize. It was almost too exciting to imagine.

Our eyes gazed upon those toys with wonderment. There were basketballs, footballs, trucks, toy dishes, dolls and doll accessories, model cars and airplanes, jewelry boxes, matchbox cars, games and things like that. The big prize, given away at the end of the drawing, was a brand new shiny bike or sled. It was always cold outside, but when a kid could get a chance to win prizes like those, it was well worth the shivering.

We gathered for that drawing every Christmas, and—out of a family with seven children—I don't remember any of us ever bringing toys home with us. But then, there was pretty stiff competition—everyone had large families back then.

Still, it was fun to have that bag of fruit and candy, and I don't think any of us were emotionally scarred from not winning any of the toys. There was always next year.

Looking back now after I've had children of my own—and helped provide for Christmases during our own tough times in agriculture, I have wondered how my parents did it. Even though Christmas was so much simpler than it seems now, it still had to challenge them financially every year.

They say the best gifts of Christmas are the memories, and I would have to agree. Money helps at Christmas time, but the heart is what gives the holiday its true meaning.

My parents did a great job of stretching their budget to include Christmas. But what they really gave us all year was a family large enough to have two teams for baseball, siblings to be our life-long friends, and discipline, common sense and a work ethic for the next generation.

Some of the best Christmas memories I have with our children involve picking out a tree. The experience changed so much as the children grew. One photo I have shows my husband and our (then) elementary-aged daughter carrying the tree we had just cut. It shows them at opposite ends of the tree, facing opposite directions, appearing to be walking.

Poor Christmas tree.

It should have been a sign of what was to come raising this group of kiddies.

IT'S A DOG'S LIFE

It's been said that to love and be loved is the greatest happiness of existence. I know that anyone who has owned a dog is sure of the truthfulness of that statement.

We got our dog, Max, when he was six weeks old. It's pretty hard not to love a little puppy, though my husband begged to differ with that on more than one occasion.

Within the first week or two that he lived with us, he somehow got into some rat poison. A call to the vet told us what to do, and luckily, Max was fine. He followed that by chewing on everything there was around—but when he chewed the lining out of a helmet that was a childhood souvenir of my husband's, Max was in more trouble than Justin Bieber. Still, he was a happy dog. I once read a sign that said, "Dogs laugh with their tails." Max's tail was always busy.

One day he found a (mostly empty) jug of weed killer to chew on and dragged it around the house yard. No one thought much about the jug sitting near the edge of the grass until the grass began dying, and in a most unusual pattern. That dang dog. Once again, a call to the vet.

They say, "You can't teach an old dog new tricks, but you can't teach a stupid dog anything." I think my husband agreed with that many times over when Max was a puppy. After about "so many" of his puppy tricks, my husband was beginning to run out of patience with him—and when he was out carousing and causing trouble one day, my husband had had it. The only reason Max lived past that day was because the school bus came, carrying our middle-school children home before he got the job done.

It was a stay of execution for Max.

As he grew out of his puppy ways, he became a friend to all of us. He would nuzzle up and want to be petted—though some of those petting sessions came rather gingerly because, as a farm dog, we knew where he had been. He always came to greet us; he would sit and watch me do the laundry, peering through the basement window of our house; he sat at the front step and guarded the farm. And at the end of a bad day, Max was always there with his affection.

I worked with someone who once said that when he had a bad day at work and people were on his case, it comforted him to know that at least his wife and his dog still loved him. Dogs believe in you, even when you don't believe in yourself—the sign of a true friend.

When Max got very old and couldn't make it up the steps anymore, we could see that his time with us was winding down. He'd been with us for more than 12 years; our children grew up with him. But now he wasn't eating and it was difficult for him to lift his head up.

Once again, a call to the vet—but this time, not to save his life, but to end his suffering.

Making those calls shake us to the core. In those times, we come to understand with greater clarity that the veterinarian's job can also be very difficult emotionally as he/she sees such raw emotion in the faces of the family who brings their pet to him/her, seeking a humane end to their suffering.

But it will only be the start of theirs.

Max's pain was ended, and his final ride home was in the back of the pickup truck he used to wait to see every day, with his tail wagging. The guys all carried him to his resting place. We stood around his grave, sharing memories with laughter and tears and saying our farewells to one of the friends we had known the longest at our farm. That corner of the yard became sacred ground. His passing brought the brevity and preciousness of life to us once again. Saying farewell always hurts, no matter how old you are, and no matter how many animals you have loved.

I read once, "A dog is the only one that loves you more than he loves himself." If it really is true that to love and be loved is the greatest happiness of existence, we hope we gave Max a happy existence with us. He gave us so much more, and we are grateful.

"In your life you will have many dogs,
but your dog will only have you."

(AUTHOR UNKNOWN)

LIFE AT THE SALE BARN

I read with interest the other day about a sale barn in Rock Island, Illinois that had closed. It made me a little sad because sale barns have long been places where dreams are made. Buyers and sellers come together, friendships are born and farmers gather as neighbors and colleagues to watch their—or someone else's—animals go through the sale ring.

I had the pleasure of watching our sons' calves sell not long ago at our local sale barn. The guys were sitting in the stands a little nervously, calculating, and hoping they would receive fair reimbursement for a year's work.

The sale barn is a place where friends meet and jokes are shared among new and old acquaintances, no matter what the ag climate is. I heard this one from a new friend I made there: "A sermon should be like a woman's skirt—long enough to cover the necessities and short enough to keep your interest."

The joke came from a man who later told me his father was able to cling to 240 acres of farm land and raise eight children through the Great Depression by making and selling whiskey on the side. It was interesting to hear about the creative genius of farmers, who love their land and will do what they have to in order to pass it down to their children someday.

The sale barn is a place where the brotherhood of farming knows no age limits—as young producers sit among the more experienced ones, listening to their jokes and stories and always, learning from them. At this sale, one man brought his dog along. Apparently, a farmer and his dog truly are inseparable, working closely together in all aspects of the cattle business.

Farmers come in coveralls and manure-covered boots. It's a sale barn, after all; everyone knows what they do for a living and no one expects them to look manicured. Or clean.

The smell of wood chips fills the air, the auctioneer begins his rhythmic call and eyes are scanning the crowd. There are maybe as many hopes as there are disappointments, as buyers and sellers have different 'fair' prices in mind for what they hope to accomplish.

The gates swing open to let the animals in and it's 100 percent focus as phones come out and calculators work quickly. Those helping the auctioneer are also focused on the crowd. We hear the loud and familiar "Yep!" as bidders are acknowledged. I once sneezed and thought I would be taking home animals I never intended to have. I'm not sure, but in all honestly I may be more of a menace than not to my husband in a place like that.

Some of the calves are sassy and kick their heels up. The first time I saw one fall down in the ring I knew what she felt like. I almost did that at my eighth grade graduation, too, when I forgot to lift up the front of my floor-length dress as I climbed the steps to the gym stage.

Poor calf—oh, the embarrassment. At least I had a dress to blame it on.

From my perspective, it was a great place to spend the afternoon—surrounded by farmers and their unique senses of humor, experiencing their positive attitudes simply because they love what they do; making new friends, seeing old friends, catching up on life and best of all—no waiting in line at the ladies' room.

That's right—be jealous, my guy farmer friends.

The local sale barn and area hog buying stations gave our family many memories that we will keep—some happy, some bittersweet and some even heart-wrenching as we watched the hog market decline in the 1990s. But those experiences defined us as a farm family, and we're still in it today.

I hope sale barns are still around by the time our children have children and can build those kinds of memories together. It's a kind of bonding that can't even be done around the dinner table, because humor and wisdom about life is often best received by children via anyone but Mom and Dad, especially the older the children get.

The sale barn is actually pretty macho stuff, even for us ladies of the farm.

THE 'PASTURE-IZED' SUPPER

It was really quite innocent. I was checking out at the grocery store one day when the cashier asked me how I got so dirty. Not realizing how much I resembled a speckle-faced sheep, it occurred to me that washing the car that day splattered plenty of its contents onto me, and was no job for the pristine-hearted.

As a family, we have eaten supper in many kids of places—the park, beside the lake, the elevator parking lot, on the road (literally), in an empty grain bin and in the mountains of Colorado. But they probably all pale by comparison to the night we ate supper in the pasture.

Harvest was in full swing. In our operation come harvest time, supper-ware grows tires and moves around from field to field in wandering gypsy fashion. The food tries to stay warm while we hunt down the people who are combining, trucking and working ground.

One night as I was tracking down my family, my husband told me where they were working and said, "...but we're not actually in the field. Were parked in the pasture."

In had just finished feeding a crew a few miles away and had decided to take the most direct route there. It led me down two miles of Level B service roads, which don't threaten me during the fall like they do in the winter. Feeling like I was headed down a cow path anyway, I tooled along in the dark with great ease, knowing I was cutting out unnecessary miles.

When I got toward the end of the second mile, it became apparent that in that area of the county they must have gotten more than the one inch of rain all summer that we got, because the water was splashing up onto the sides of the car, and I was gunning it so I didn't get stuck.

I arrived at the pasture and saw the trucks and combine lights. As I got closer I slowly made my way through cows that looked at both me and the car with a hint of tranquil suspicion. Their distrust of me was painfully evident as they never once broke their icy stares.

I was getting supper out of the back of the car when my husband came over, wondering where I'd been four-wheeling, visually examining the car with the same look the cows had.

I was beginning to feel a little unwelcome.

The plot thickened as I dished up the main entrée—meatloaf. As the cows began to close in on us I began to wish I had cooked something with chicken or pork that night. The cows knew where the beef was, and were starting to have one with me. I'm certain they counted their pasture mates to ensure they were all there and not on our plates.

We scarfed our supper that night in front of a critical four-legged audience which had gathered around us like a common street gang. And when it was time to go I realized I'd stepped in a pie, but not one I had brought.

Great.

I wiped that off my shoe in the pasture grass as best I could. The tires had also found plenty of it on the way in and out of the pasture, and it became obvious that the car was going to need to be washed after that evening's unusual harvest catering festivities.

Thus, my speckled face, hands, arms and clothing as I checked out at the grocery store the next day. Unless they could smell me, I bet they thought it was all road grime.

Our car could have used some actual pasteurization to rid itself of objectionable content following our supper in the pasture.

Welcome to the farm.

MOVING THE BARN

I had the amazing opportunity to be present when a young family moved a barn onto their farm this past fall. The barn was at least 103 years old by the family's best estimate.

The father of the young family was the youngest of four boys who grew up on the farm to where the barn was coming. I stood by his father and we talked about the fact that his young grandchildren were taking the morning off from school to be part of their family's history.

"They'll remember this all their lives," he said, as he looked up at the barn and continued on about its construction in a time when technology was not what it is today. "I think of all the wood that was cut by hand, and the people who built this barn."

The excitement was building for everyone there as the mover said it was time to start.

"It's quite a job you have there," I said to him.

He smiled, continued his work and replied, "It's just a job."

But to family and friends there that day, it was obvious that it was far more than just a job—it was a team of people delivering both the past and the present; delivering history and now a future for an old building that may have otherwise fallen into disrepair over time, being unused and outdated, and eventually forgotten, dismantled and buried.

The barn slowly came off of its century-long foundation, did a U-turn in the grove and exited the abandoned farm place via a soybean field. It was something to see.

The barn seemed to glide, with the help of a large quad-track tractor pulling the moving truck and the barn through the black gold that is Iowa field soil. What a striking sight—seeing a modern tractor slowly pull more than 100 years of history behind it.

The cows grazed in the nearby pasture, unaware that something big was happening.

I thought of all the things that could have gone on in the barn in 100 years. Back in the day, farm families often built the barn before they built the house on the homestead—so yes, some people really were born in a barn. I thought of the animals that were tended to there, the grain that was picked by hand (or threshed) and stored there, desperate prayers for rain, and private, tearful prayers for restored human health for a loved one—or asking God 'why.' And back in the day, even some child disciplining most likely went on out in the barn.

Yes, a barn was part of a family.

I thought about the cost and the labor with the technology and tools they had to build such a monstrous structure ... and wondered what it would cost to build a replica today.

Finally the barn made its way out on to the gravel road and its true size was plain to see. It dwarfed the vehicles that had dotted the quiet country road ahead of it, and slowly made its way through, with cameras clicking and people watching with great anticipation, as if the barn were to be revered.

The giant structure seemed almost personified as it neared its new home. I was imagining it being happy to be with a family again who would restore and care for it.....to have life breathed back into it after so many years of abandonment. And to once again house animals and grain. It would be re-purposed, in a manner of speaking.

As the barn slowly and steadily made its way onto its new home, I asked the owner if he had overdosed on antacids yet. We moved a house a few years ago.

I remembered.

"As long as she keeps moving, I'm okay," he said with a nervous smile.

The movers delivered the barn, and the barn delivered the anchor to the farm. And it was plain to see that everything was good.

Our son had driven by in the midst of it all to check the cows in the nearby pasture.

"Only in Iowa do you get stuck waiting because there's a barn on the road," he joked, openly proud of his own Iowa heritage.

WHEN YOU'RE AS OLD AS A TOWN

I don't mean to say I'm old, but it's hard to dispute the fact that when I was born there were people alive who were probably living at the time of the Civil War. But if you go blabbing that secret, I will have to hunt you down and flog you with a wet corn stalk.

I'm serious.

And just between you and me, this year while on vacation in Florida I ordered from the "55-Plus" menu for the first time. Ever. I thought it would feel great to save a little money, and although it mostly bruised my ego, I guessed the small savings was nice. But after that meal I chose to go back to the beach and stick my head back into the ocean sand.

I didn't want to know I was old enough for that.

I knew a lady from a neighboring town who made it to the ripe old age of 104—she almost made it to 105. She was a spunky farm wife in the day, and there wasn't a blade of grass that grew under her busy feet—not even in her later years. She could work circles around anyone. She was part coon dog and could smell trouble brewing, and could see it coming from afar since she had lived around those parts for 60 years.

She kept her family going, as mothers do—and without any lip from her children or anyone else who knew her. And what she said, went.

We laid that spirited woman to rest last spring, and at her funeral luncheon a man approached me with some memories of her.

He also told me as we talked that their town was 125 years old. Then he said something that really made me think.

He said, "...do you know that she was almost as old as the town?" Sheesh. That sounds old ... to be almost as old as a town.

Iowa Secretary of Agriculture Bill Northey had once told me about an elderly farmer who traveled to Des Moines to have his century farm recognized. As the man approached with his walker, Northey congratulated him. The man replied, with teary eyes, "I've been waiting 50 years for this day."

He had willingly contributed the sweat and grit that farm life demands, and the years went by almost unnoticed. He said farewell over time to his involvement with the farming, but not to his love of the farm. It took the use of a walker, but he made it to the stage that acknowledged what he had worked for all of his life. And with his fifth generation farmers standing there with him, he knew his life's work would continue, and also be his legacy.

The centenarian generation is our true "information superhighway" – today's living legends. The internet can tell us much of what we need to know, but those people can tell us things the internet cannot because they have lived life and come out on the other side of the storms. They are our direct connection to history—stories of their hard work, hard ways, hard luck, and lessons they learned the hard way---which was often the only way.

They know.

They now look at real life through the lens of hindsight. One hundred years of it.

If you ever have the chance to sit at the feet of a centenarian (or of any old-timer) and visit, do yourself the favor of having that conversation. And not just once. It's important for everyone—but certainly for the farming community—to carry those stories of tenacity and determination from the past into the future. We face adversities today, but those people faced some unimaginable trials and lived to tell us about it. They can be a source of strength for us.

They are our original reference guide for true grit, problem solving and ingenuity.

When you're almost as old as a town, there's plenty to tell ... and plenty to learn.

Even if you were born just short of 100 years after the Civil War ended.

BEANWALKERS WANTED: DEAD OR ALIVE

Probably one of the greatest tragedies of our day is the fact that farmers and their families no longer walk beans.

Oh, how I used to long to be my cousin from New York who never had to perform such menial labor. While visiting us once when we were growing up, she even dared to ask us what bean walking was. My sister and I looked at each other with utter surprise. We thought everyone walked beans.

We showed her, and she nearly fainted.

I recently went out to read the gas meter and crossed through part of a bean field to get there. It brought back memories that I now cherish, but at the time, came disguised in sweat, corn knives, wet beans, sweat bees and coveted water jugs at the end of the row to mark where we'd been. Everyone drank from the same jug—and we all lived to tell about it.

Walking beans was a job we did with mostly with Dad, who kept an eye not only on his rows but the rows of seven children who weren't as jazzed about the job as he seemed to be. He wanted weeds pulled most often, which was fine until you came to a big sunflower with those prickly stems.

To this day I will never understand a sunflower motif in a farm kitchen. My hands hated those things—along with sticky milk weeds and those obnoxious-smelling button weeds.

How I despised being out in the bean field at 7 a.m., with a cold ride to the field in the back of the pickup, the wet bean leaves that made my pant legs, shoes and socks wet first thing, and the damp soil that made wedge shoes out of any pair of tennis shoes we wore.

It's how my sisters and I learned how to walk in high heels.

Dad would sometimes remind us of the job we were there for when things got chatty. We would hear, "...a little less talkin' and a little more walkin.'"

He also carried a hoe so he could reach over the rows to get what everyone else was missing. Now and then he'd tap you on the head with his hoe handle and use it to show you that you missed one 'back there.'

We hired out and got plenty of experience, once walking a field that had so much corn in it that we all took one row and used corn knives. Dad finally got us out of that job—there was just so much corn. We couldn't believe that even Dad thought it was too much to do.

There was the time a farmer lost his prized pliers in the bean field and offered a reward to the one who found them. Of course my brother found the pliers—but they were in my rows.

There was the time we had walked beans for a neighbor on a very hot and humid afternoon. We took a needed break and my brothers climbed into a nearby tree for some shade and rest—and you might know that the farmer and his wife showed up at that same time with lunch for us. It looked bad, but they understood.

Looking back, they were some of the best times we had growing up together. We were each others' captive audience—sentenced to four rows each, next to each other, half a mile at a time before turning around to walk four more rows each to the other end of the field, and all across the width of the field. Every morning. Most afternoons. Sometimes in the evenings if it was cool and there was a lot to do.

We learned about each other—our hopes and dreams, the things that were going on, exchanging jokes, telling stories, wondering together, running to the end rows when it began to rain, dirt clod fights and corn butt fights—even some arguing and name calling among siblings.

They truly were the best of times and the worst of times...but now I wouldn't trade that experience for anything. But sad as it is that farm families don't do that anymore, I'm also glad.

I'm not *that* grateful for the memories.

MOTHERS OF STEEL

Whether in town or on the farm, there is hardly any mistaking the notion that mothers have a big job to do. They have held families together since, well, the invention of mothers.

For some mothers the job is no big deal—we see that even out in the barns. Those moms lie around like it's just another day, chewing their cud and digging in the manure. But then, many of those moms can stand up and have their babies, turn around and sniff them, lick them off, then wander off to see what there is to eat.

I totally get that.

Farm mothers are truly mothers of steel—they have to be for the kind of lives they live. Her life involves many different seasons, not just the usual four, and they all have to do with the work that has to be done outside. She can't plan a thing more than a day or two in advance, and some times of the year even that is too early to plan ahead.

Darn weather.

And meals—not only are they served at unlikely times of the day and night, but every now and then she'll have a kid that squawks about what's on the menu. If you were me, you would be told by your busy mother, "If you don't like it, supper's over." (And mean it.)

We all learned to eat what she put in front of us, and ate it without even sniffing it first.

And when we would ask, "What's for supper?" She would reply, "Whatever you fix."

That's how my sisters and I learned to cook.

My mother—a city girl all of her growing-up years—had a lot to learn about being a farm wife and mother at first. She had to learn how to clean chickens—a necessary and stinky job that no one I know ever enjoyed. I'll bet she was reading the fine print in her wedding vows with great fervor after she did that job for the first time.

She had to mend blue jeans for a family of nine, and I don't know how she did it without an arm on her sewing machine. Maybe there was a reason why she needed to spend so much time out in the wash house when she was doing that job—maybe seeking liquid coping skills.

She would say to me, "Dad wears his denim shirts so long and they get so thin that you can almost read through them." Great Depression-era kids never forgot what it was like to have nothing.

She had to watch her sons learn how to use tractors and implements, and pray that they would be safe once they got going on their own following a few instructions from Dad. She closed the kitchen curtains on silo filling day because she couldn't stand watching my brothers walk around on top of the silo. She went head to head with my brother's knee that had been torn open by an angry sow.

Yes, nerves of steel.

She fed hungry baling and corn shelling crews without so much as a microwave oven or a cake mix. Talk about gutsy.

Now and then my brothers would brawl it out on the living room floor. Mom would come in with a broom, give them a few good swats with it and holler, "Take your fight outside!" (She didn't ask them to stop fighting ... she just didn't want her living room to look like a frat house on Sunday morning.)

And it may have been a subliminal message she sent me once as she fixed my well-loved Raggedy Ann doll that suffered an accidental leg-ectomy. When I got the doll back, the leg was sewn on backwards. I didn't know if she was that busy or if it was a silent message about possible consequences for my future behaviors. The doll is still that way today, reminding me that I always need to keep my toes pointed in the same direction.

Carry on, farm moms everywhere---your hearts are made of both love...and steel.

ARE YOU BUSY?

It's a question many a farm wife has heard over the years. It's an honest question, and yet it stirs up a little consternation when her husband comes in while she's clearly busy working on something and asks her, "Are you busy?"

It can be a rather threatening feeling since we don't always know what kind of help is needed, how long our help will be needed, what we'll smell like when we come back in, or if we'll still be friends after working together. (Oh, the hog loading stories...)

I read that a chicken can run up to speeds of nine miles per hour when it feels threatened. Nonetheless—threatened or not by that question—farm wives (instead of scampering away with chicken-like speed) typically face the music and grab their work gloves.

Whenever my husband asks for my help, I often think of a conversation we once had while out traveling. I saw a sign that pointed to Leavenworth, Kansas, and said, "Hey—you want to stop and do a little hard labor while we're out and about?"

My husband replied, "We have that in Milford."

In my speaking travels I met a woman who told me her husband was having trouble getting his arm into the business end of a sow to pull her pigs, so he asked her if she would do it. She was grossed out at the thought, but she mustered up all of her courage to stick her arm in there that first time, because she knew her smaller arm would probably get the job done.

I'm pretty sure I would have lost my cookies right there on the spot.

Her husband tried to encourage her by saying, "Just think of them as $50 bills." She told him she didn't mind $50 bills, but, "... these counterfeits *(dead pigs)* have to go.'"

I said to her of the experience, "Well, you lived to tell about it, didn't you?"

She said, "Yes I did—and so did he."

Oh, sometimes farmers walk a fine line in asking for their wives' help.

Farm women abide by a lot of unwritten rules. "Everything else comes first" is often the first and foremost one, as she learns to stop what she's doing on a dime to help outside. She sorts and loads livestock, keeps track of the breeding schedule, runs farm equipment, learns how to vaccinate and knows not to hesitate when she hears, "Call the vet!" She learns that an open gate can only bring bad news, and does the housework whenever she's not at her job in town, in the field or out in the livestock yards. She keeps records, the books and the peace.

A young girl I know who grew up in town was dating a farm hand and was beginning to understand the constraints that farm life can place on relationships. There is always something that needs to be done, and 5:00 is a far cry from quitting time. After all, the sun is still out.

When we were once visiting about farm life, she asked, "Will I always come second?"

I understood that. I was her more than three decades earlier, and I even grew up on a farm.

Coming second is the nature of the beast, especially if there is a crop to plant or harvest, or hay to bale and put away before the rain. Farm babies in the barn take precedence over everything, as do livestock chores, which literally never go away. It's the nature of the beast, and in time, the farm woman understands that. When that young lady works her first ground she'll understand what her farmer feels when he's out there in his own little slice of heaven.

I said to her, "You just need to be patient with that."

I didn't have the heart to tell her she'll really come in third. No farm wife I know ever ranked ahead of her husband's pair of pliers.

And she better bring a pair with her outside when he asks her if she's busy. She'll probably need them while doing her share of the hard labor out there.

THE BEST OF TIMES, THE WORST OF TIMES

First of all, let me just say that the Schwallers are a wrestling family. Farmers have a good chance of raising successful wrestlers because every day is weightlifting day on the farm.

Wrestling does wonders for a mother's prayer life—especially when her son wrestles heavyweight at 210 pounds, and faces someone on the mat who weighs all of 285 pounds. He used to hear jokes that his opponent was "... tied up out behind their school bus, eating from the bunk."

It often seemed biblical in nature. While I never snuck a slingshot into my purse to use from the stands in case our son needed a little help with all those Goliaths he faced, there were days I thought (with that kind of weight difference and ferocious take-down velocity) I would only need a spatula go scrape him off of the mat.

Even though the letters for the heavyweight bracket read, "HWT," our son wrestled some whose weights could have been measured by "CWT." Still, we learned through his experience that size doesn't always matter. He held his own. He was a strong farm kid.

Wrestlers have seen the sign at the sectional meet saying, "The Road to Des Moines Begins Here." It helps them remember why they are there. Physics class comes to the mat.

Once they make it to the district meet, they're close enough to a state tournament berth to taste it, but far enough away that it will still be a fight. Emotions run high at district wrestling meets. Nervous stomachs ensue. It's the whole enchilada--it's the top two places or nothing, and every wrestler came wanting one of those two places. Only a few would move on.

Wrestlers pace the floor with great anxiety--focused, knowing what they have to do. The National Anthem is played, and everyone in the gym becomes one people under one flag if only for a few minutes, before splitting back into school districts. I'm certain God is very busy hearing prayers at that time. Former wrestlers there remember that exciting and awful rock-in-the-gut feeling.

Once it begins, the gym comes alive. Wrestlers have six minutes at a time to make their dreams happen. Bodies get slammed, arms get twisted, wrestlers sometimes lie injured on the mat and parents' hearts leap into their throats. Noses bleed and eyes are blackened. Coaches watch the clock and yell back, "Short time!"

Brackets begin to take shape. Overtime matches are intense, especially in the finals round. Everyone wants to be the best in the district, then take it to Wells Fargo Arena.

Wrestlers in the consolation brackets still have a chance to get to Des Moines. Wrestle-backs are the longest possible road to Des Moines, and winning in that way can be just as sweet. But losing that way hurts just a little more. Those kids wrestle with the most heart.

When district wrestlers fall short of the mark, they might lie on the mat for a moment, letting (what just happened) soak in— while the crowd for the winner is cheering wildly all around him. He knows it's his loss, and his loss alone. And so it is in the sport of wrestling.

Yet, he gets up, shakes the hand of his opponent and leaves the mat—and his state wrestling dream that he worked toward all year--behind. Some leave for a season, and some for the last time ever if they are seniors. It can be heart-wrenching to watch. Wrestling fans share in their pain.

Close only counts in horseshoes---and sometimes in wrestling. Our family has experienced both sides of that coin—advancement overjoy and heartbreaking loss--sometimes at the same time, with two boys in wrestling. Following a large, prestigious tournament one day when one of our sons came home a champion and the other left the mat after a gut-wrenching disqualification in the finals, someone told us, "I wouldn't want to be you tonight."

It was hard to know what to do once we got home.

Advancing at districts is surreal. It's been a season—or many years—of work to get there, and a sweaty hug between coaches and wrestlers says what words cannot say—for both.

John Wayne spoke wise words when he said, "Courage is being scared to death, and saddling up anyway." Wrestlers know that. The sport also demands John Wayne-like 'true grit' from young people who dare to take on a sport that can be so life-giving, and so unforgiving.

It can be the best of times....and also the worst of times. Just ask any wrestler.

Or any wrestler's mother.

THOSE CRAZY GOATS

Fair time is winding down around the state, and with each passing year I am amazed at the number of kids who put the time in to take animals to the county fair.

It's usually the sheep show that entertains me the most. Some sheep have been worked with so much that they could practically be present at the family table on a chair instead of a platter. Others have to be dragged in and out of the show ring, head down and feet dug in, skidding all the way in and out. It's reminiscent of taking my husband to the dentist, except for that "skidding out" part. He'll gladly race out of a dentist's office.

Our boys decided one winter they wanted to take goats to the fair. Our farm at the time was indigenous to sheep, and as livestock went, had only otherwise seen hogs (not counting the occasional mouse sightings in the house). My husband really didn't want to start raising goats, but told them that if they could find somewhere to put them, they could do it.

It was the last anyone had ever spoken about it—that is, until the day of spring weigh-ins. My husband was on the committee and was helping at the scale. Someone backed a trailer up to the barn and unloaded some goats, and was talking to my husband as if they belonged to our sons. Of course, my husband disagreed, never having seen them before.

Enter our two (then) high school sons, who showed up to help unload the trailer. Turns out the goats were theirs indeed—and there was even a third one that belonged to a friend of theirs. They'd been keeping them at the neighbor's instead of finding a place for them at home.

They really pulled one over on their dad and everyone got a good laugh out of it.

By fair time the goats needed to be groomed. Never having done this before, our boys got the clippers out and went to work. The first goat (belonging to their friend, who was there with them) received somewhat of an Army-style 'do. The first pass— right down the middle of its back—was pretty short; almost down to the skin. After being horrified at their first pass at goat barbering, they conferred extensively and decided there was no hiding or fixing it, and there was nothing else to do but to groom the rest of the goat in that same fashion.

Oh, the humiliation of that goat, having to go streaking at the fair right in front of God and the judge.

They paid more attention to the clipper adjustments on the other two goats, and continued on. When the day of the goat show arrived, all three took their goats out into the show ring—the only goats of the whole show, wouldn't you know.

The guys stood nervously in front of the judge, thinking about the bad clip job on their friend's goat, and feeling bad about it. They were lined up according to the judge's approval, and he picked up the microphone. Though he said many things about their goats, the only thing we remembered hearing was that he really liked the way their friend's goat was groomed. Our family was all trying to suppress our laughter—in the show ring and in the stands alike.

It's never been our style to have done something wrong, and still have it be right.

The following year, another friend of theirs also had a goat that she kept at our place, and came over to have it groomed during the week of the fair. Our sons got out their clippers once again—now that they knew what they were doing—and set up for the job.

When one of our sons took the halter off of the goat, it took off running full speed across the pen as it had done countless times before. It usually stopped just short of the concrete wall and would turn around. This time it didn't remember to stop, and ran head-first into the wall.

The wall won, and it was a permanent K-O for the goat.

"It was the damndest thing I ever saw," our son said, adding that they were all stunned at what had just occurred right before their eyes....and just days before the fair was to start.

That goat was probably a kamikaze pilot in a previous life...or maybe just a scapegoat. Either way, it really got their goat that it up and died just days before the fair.

One the other hand, maybe anything was better to that goat than the fear of appearing nearly naked before a crowd of scrupulous onlookers. There's more than one way to skin a goat.

Well, kind of.

MEMOIRS OF A YOUNG FARM MOTHER

It doesn't take very long for a first-time mother—urban or rural--to lose track of all the lofty goals she once had about being the perfect mother and homemaker.

We went from one to three children in two pregnancies. We'd seen multiple births out in the barns all the time, but now it had come to the house. And our house resembled a barn for many months afterward as I navigated my way through cloth diapers for two, projectile spit-up, chocolate chip cookie slobber on high chairs and in hair; small plastic building pieces hidden in the carpet; chair and blanket forts, "sale barn" set-up days, implements strewn about the kitchen and living room, and being yelled at as I carried the overflowing laundry basket through the living room with a toddler shouting, "Mom! You're walking on our corn field!"

And I had never repeated myself so many times in a day. It was only an inkling of what was to come as I entered my 50s, but that I wouldn't be able to blame that on the kids.

I handled so many dirty diapers with twins that when my husband announced he was going to have urea put on (his fields), it sounded more like a medical condition.

After all of that diaper rinsing in the toilet, I was surprised by one of our sons who, (when older and helping clean up the shop one day), came to me with a handkerchief held by a pair of pliers. Suspecting a sprinkling of raccoon doo-doo or some other atrocity associated with it, I asked him what was on it. His only reply was, "I don't know....boogers or something."

Even I—a girl--could pick up something as mysterious as a pair of compression shorts off of his bedroom floor (without pliers), sniff them to determine the caliber of cleanliness and decide what to do with them. After all, I've smelled way worse than that on the farm.

Farm wives and moms get used to terrible smells everywhere. In fact, terrible smells seem to follow her family members wherever they are due to the nature of their work.

I remember coming home from our county fairgrounds late one night after preparing for the kids' first 4H sheep show the next morning. Everyone was exhausted and the kids were all piled on top of one another, sleeping in the back seat of the pickup on the way home.

I noticed an obnoxious smell about halfway home and asked, "What reeks in here?"

My husband tiredly replied, "I think it's us."

Probably my most annoying memory of having young children is when we stopped to visit a friend of mine who had just retired from his job in town. Our boys were 18 months old and our daughter was 3-½ years old at the time. They were all behaving fairly well, thus, the guts to bring them all to his acreage to be set free for a few minutes before we went home.

Let me preface this by saying I had become a stay-home mother when our twins were born. We went without some things in order to be able to afford it, since there would have been three in daycare.

My husband worked a full-time job in town in order to keep his farming dream alive, so I was doing a solo job of mothering and parenting most of the time during those baby and toddler years as well. Much like farming, it was a relentless job that never ended— especially on days when everyone was ill and the "sick laundry" piled up while kids needed to be held, comforted and cared for; when the diaper pail was overflowing, when they could tip a cart over in the grocery store, when Mother Nature called in stores, when everyone needed to eat and I didn't feel like cooking, and especially after all of the children could out run me.

I swear that toddlers could sweep the gold medal stands at Olympic track events.

My friend said to me as we were visiting, "...so, how do you like loafing?"

I'm pretty sure the look on my face must have been the reason for his back-peddling.

I'm also pretty sure it was the last time he uttered those words to a young mother.

HARVESTING THE HUMOR

And now, a few thoughts about the funny things the harvest teaches us about life:

- **When you don't know what you're doing, everyone else does.** It's the age-old standard about small town life, but it also applies to life in the field. There is no hiding a grain cart boombie – everyone can see that pile of corn on the ground next to the truck.

  Usually that ill-placed pile is along a main highway, of course.

- **Enough with the scales.** The farm wife does enough to battle the bathroom scale, let alone now having to manage the scale in the grain cart tractor and at the elevator. More than once this harvest season as we were hauling to the bins and keeping track of volume, my husband asked, "Did you write your weight down?"

  He's lucky we were harvesting.

- **If you are driving wagons, a grain cart or a truck, there is always someone waiting to dump on you.** Although this kind of dumping is in the literal sense, and is necessary for the job to be completed, I think I'm pretty safe to say that many a farm wife has been 'dumped on' in the 'yelling' sense, by a frustrated—even perhaps a well-meaning—son of the soil. A farm wife I know decided one day not to take it from her husband—she walked away from her field duties in the midst of their short-handed harvest, not to return for the rest of the day.

She was like the Statue of Liberty for farm wives everywhere that day.

- **Maturity isn't for weenies.** I can tell from my mission in the corn fields that these stalks that once were green and lush are now brown and stripped of height and leaves from old age and the wind. It's a ghastly reminder of what isn't that far away for me. Seeing the shriveled remains of the near-naked stalks also reminded me that we were out of prunes.

- **The tassel still reigns.** The tassel's main job of pollinating is relatively short-lived, but nonetheless, important. But what's it supposed to do after it has fulfilled its duties? It switches roles, that's what. It becomes a pointy crown on top of the stalk. So when the pollen has all been distributed, she straightens her crown and hangs on for the season-long wild ride.

- **Finding each other in life can be a challenge. But out in the field it is necessary.** We were harvesting in a field that was quite hilly this year, and after I finished loading the truck, I started my trek back to the combine, only to find that it appeared I was in the field alone. A simple, "Marco!" into the radio resulted in a reply of "Polo!" as my husband came over the crest of the hill. Who says hide-and-seek games are only for the kiddies?

- **Tractor clutches could be the next big thing in fitness.** During harvest I have to stretch out when loading the trucks to keep the clutch and brake where they need to be. If I had started that job in the fourth grade like our sons did, imagine how sleek my thighs would be by now.

    I've had incidents in the fields over the years that have made my hams pucker and tighten up on demand, too. At this rate I'll have my bikini body in time for my 70th birthday. They don't give these farm fitness jobs to chimps.

- **Some chocolate in the tractor is a little slice of heaven.**
- **Some chocolate in the tractor is Satan.**
- **Sometimes cussing is just plain necessary.**

And from the files of, *"How Can I Occupy My Mind While Waiting For the Combine to Fill?"* A couple of jokes:

- What kind of dishes you give to a farmer? *(Corningware)*
- How far in rank a farmer can go in the military? *(Kernel)*

And you didn't think you'd learn anything by reading this book, did you?

IS IT SOUP YET?

Let me preface this piece by saying that our children would certainly have starved over the years if my husband had not cooked for them in my absence.

Many were the summers when they were out of school and I was at work, and as kids do, they would get hungry and need sustenance. Luckily, my husband was working around the farm often and could play the role of chef during the day, often with leftovers.

Let me also say that after our children left home it was a struggle to learn how to reduce the amount of food we needed at our meals. It had been so many years of needing full-sized pans of casseroles, with three hungry men in the house to feed. So in those days after we first became empty-nesters—and even some today—we open the door and examine the contents of the refrigerator only to find things we can't positively identify. They may be furry or not furry by the time we unearth them, but the long and short of it is that it appears we need to rotate the food supply more often with just two of us to use up all the groceries.

One day my husband found himself with a little extra time when he was feeding the children, and decided he would use up some of the food in the refrigerator to make soup for supper. My father used to do that. He came from "the old country," as he would say, and was good at making something out of nothing. Depression-era people learned how to do that if they were going to survive. If Dad found ten things in the refrigerator to use, he'd call it "Number

Ten Soup;" if he found only six items, it would be "Number Six Soup." You get the picture. And if unexpected company would drop by, he'd say jokingly, "We'll just put more water in the soup."

My husband found all the secret ingredients he needed to make his soup that day—meat, vegetables and all the flavorings, being careful to sidestep the celery he can't seem to swallow. He does like to experiment with his foods, and sometimes it turns out pretty great.

When I returned home from work that day I smelled soup cooking in the crock pot. It smelled delicious and I asked him what he put in it. He ran down the list of things he put in, and then it came. He didn't even know he had just tattled on himself.

"I put in a box of barley."

My eyes widened and my eyebrows raised. "A box of barley?" I inquired, not because I didn't like it, but because of its innate ability to thicken. He affirmed that I heard him correctly.

Oh boy.

My suspicions turned into reality as we dined on the soup that first night. It was awesome, flavorful and had lots of body because of the barley.

The second night we ate it, it was a thick stew.

The third night we ate it, it was a casserole.

And if there had been a fourth serving, I'm pretty sure we would have been carving our initials in the stone it would have morphed into by then. Maybe it would have even made good insulation for our home ... or maybe a sidewalk.

But far be it from me to criticize his cooking kafoozeldies—especially when he has had to do the 'scoop of shame' following some of my grain cart unloading catastrophes in the field. And right along the highway, no less, where everyone can see.

It would appear that grains have generated great strife for both of us from time to time, whether they are unloaded from an auger or from a cardboard box out of the cupboard.

In this instance, asking, "Is it soup yet?" was asked not because the soup was in the process of being made, but because it was in the process of turning into marble. It was only available to eat by spoon for a short time, followed by knives and forks, and then by air hammers.

I won't tell you about the fish dish I made one night after we were first married. There's just no need to bring that up.

MEMORIES OF A BEGINNING FARMER

This past fall my view of harvest changed from being the person who brings out a hot meal each night, to not only doing that—but driving the grain cart as well.

My view from the tractor cab also gave me a new perspective on the work and life of a farmer and his family, even though I have spent my life on the farm.

My husband started out humbly in his vocation—beginning as a hired man at the ripe old age of 14. He lived in town at the time, coming to work each day on his moped. Eventually he worked up to buying his first pickup truck.

As a high school junior he moved out to the farm where he would (years later) bring his new bride and raise his children. There, he instilled the love of the land and livestock in all of his children—something that gave him more pride than his chest could hold.

But it took time. He started out in the 1980s, of all times, with a few hogs and a dream. With no farm land to raise feed for them, he bought every kernel of corn that went into them during a scary time in ag history. It was careful livestock and financial management that moved him forward far enough to buy a skid loader. What a relief to pitch the pitch fork.

When he bought his first tractor—a Farmall Super M, it was a day to celebrate. That followed with the purchase of a 190 Allis Chalmers and a few small, well-used implements to groom and plant the first quarter of land he was able to acquire in the early 1990s.

He worked seven days a week—including full time factory work in town for five years and farming part time to realize his "someday" dream of farming full time. He never lost sight of his dream. It was something to witness that kind of fierce tenacity and drive.

As opportunities arose and newer equipment replaced the old, some of the older machines took a home in the grove. It's hard to get rid of some pieces of machinery—like his first combine. Someone once asked him what he used for a combine, and when he said it was a '95 John Deere, they said, "Oh—a 9500..." He said, "Nope—a 95."

Their looks of surprise were usually pretty amusing. No one farmed with those anymore.

When a traveling junk dealer gazed upon it once and came to buy it, my husband could not part with it. The combine was his earliest memory of prosperity, and he couldn't sell it to a junk dealer. It was hydrostatic, awesome, and it did everything he needed done. And there was a time when that combine was "the next big thing" him and our children.

There were financial pitfalls and heartaches on the way to farming full time—including the need to liquidate a sow herd once, and the farm crisis of 1998, which almost stole his dream from him. I would see him cry when he opened the hog check. Those were hard days.

But this fall as I drove the tractor and grain cart down the field to meet my husband in the combine, I watched as one of our loaded semis headed down the road. He had purchased this one from a man he once worked for, and then with. I thought about all of the work and heartache he endured in all those years to get where he is today.

From a rear-view mirror's perspective, a dream is never truly lost until you stop working toward it, no matter what obstacles stand in the way. He was not willing to give up. But that's the way farmers are. They have invested too much blood, sweat and tears...if not money they don't have...and time spent dreaming and planning.

I watched as our sons harvested a field across the road from where we were working one day, and thought about the dream that was for my husband and for our sons. It meant a lifetime of working toward that goal for all of them. Not every farm family can accomplish that.

For the two percent of the population who make farming their life's work, it has been, more times than not, quite a scratch-filled climb to the top. But it makes the view from there all the sweeter. That is, If you can see it through the blood, sweat...and yes, the tears.

Author Karen Schwaller lives in Milford, Iowa with her husband on their family farm. Their three children are grown and all work in agriculture. They have a foreign exchange daughter, Jana Scholze, from Germany, who lived with the family during the 2005-2006 school year, and still remains an active part of their family. Karen has been a writer and photographer all of her adult life, writing news, human interest stories and columns for various publications in Northwest Iowa on both a full-time and freelance basis. She especially enjoys writing and speaking about farm life and rural living, and all the gifts and challenges it presents.

Made in the USA
Middletown, DE
01 November 2022

13846372R00116